MORE
Metal
clay for
beaders

18 Innovative Projects

Irina Miech

Photography © 2007 Kalmbach Publishing Co.

Printed in the United States

11 10 09 08 07   1 2 3 4 5

These designs are for your personal use. They are not intended for resale.
Visit our Web site at **kalmbachbooks.com**
Secure online ordering available

Publisher's Cataloging-in-Publication Data
(Prepared by The Donohue Group, Inc.)

Miech, Irina.
　More metal clay for beaders : 18 innovative projects / Irina Miech.
　　p. : ill. ; cm.
　Includes bibliographical references.
　ISBN: 978-0-87116-242-7
　1. Jewelry making. 2. Precious metal clay. 3. Beads–Design and construction.
　4. Silver jewelry. I. Title.

TT212 .M543 2007
745.594/2

Introduction

When I was a little girl, the books in my house always were filled with dried leaves – reminders of nature, my first love. From the start, organic elements have figured prominently in my jewelry designs, but once I began working with Precious Metal Clay, I was intrigued by how precisely metal clay could capture the beauty of nature. In my first book, *Metal Clay for Beaders*, I presented a variety of step-by-step metal clay projects, many of which featured natural elements and themes. I've continued exploring the possibilities of metal clay since then, and, although I've continued to incorporate organic themes, I've also been experimenting with other techniques. The projects in this book include many natural elements – leaves, flowers, pods, and seashells. I've also included projects that use traditional jewelry-making techniques: wirework, wire-wrapping, and, of course, beading. I hope you enjoy using this book.

– *Irina Miech*

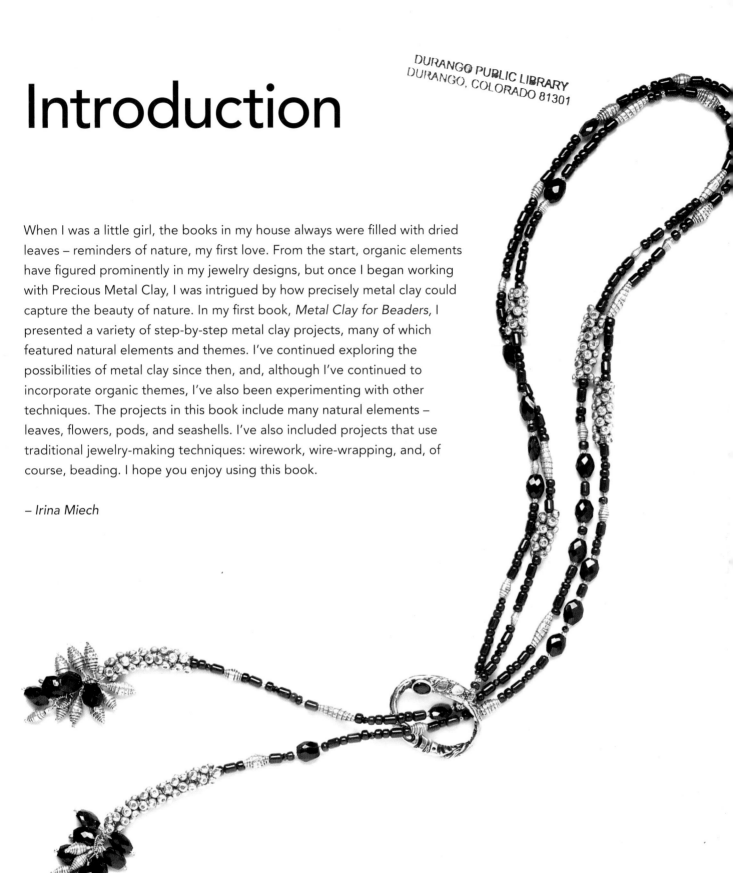

Contents

Intermediate Projects

Materials and Tools

Beginner
Projects

We start with eight projects that require a minimum of time, skills, and materials, yet produce stunning results. If you are new to metal clay, I recommend that you work through the projects in the order they are presented. You may find it helpful to consult our Materials and Tools overview that starts on p. 100 as well. As you progress through the book, your skills and confidence will grow, right along with a beautiful collection of beaded silver jewelry. If you have been working with metal clay for a while, enjoy paging through and choosing any projects that catch your interest or stretch your abilities.

Each project teaches a different metal clay technique. Once you master the technique by completing the project shown, many possibilities are open to you. Starting on p. 40 is a gallery section that shows just a few examples of my variations on the theme of each project. It is my hope that you will be inspired to take my ideas further, creating lovely and original designs of your own.

Textured Earrings

More ideas p. 40

Imprinting metal clay is a wonderful way for beginners to experiment with textures, whether the textures come from natural objects, such as leaves and flowers, or from texture sheets and rubber stamp mats. Stamp mats like the one shown here are especially easy to use. They also provide a continuous design, without a beginning, end, or borders, allowing beginners to choose the shapes and sizes of components and placement of holes without having to follow a particular design.

Make the textured components

1 Prepare your tools and materials (see p. 104). Roll the clay to the thickness of four cards if you are using a stamp mat with a standard thickness. If your stamp mat is thicker or has a deep texture, roll the clay to the thickness of five cards.

2 Use a round clay cutter to punch out a circle.

3 Apply extra Badger Balm to one side of the circle and place it on the rubber stamp mat, oiled side down. Roll the circle out to a three-card thickness (subtracting one card from the original number for a mat of regular thickness, and two cards for an extra-deep mat).

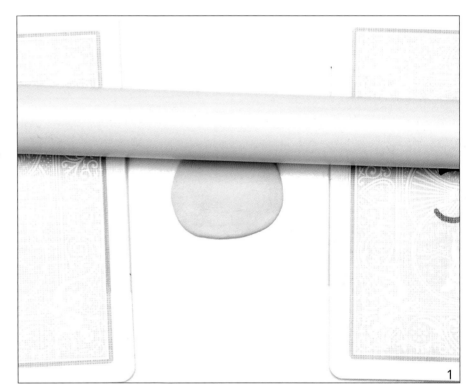

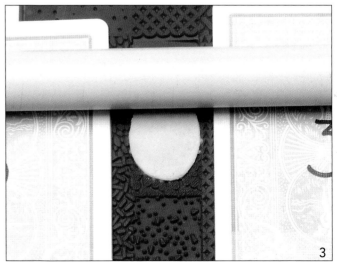

4

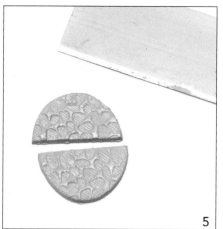

5

6

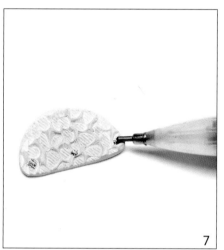

7

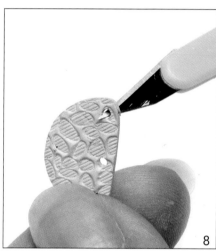
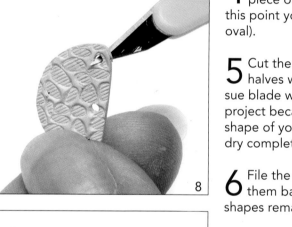

8

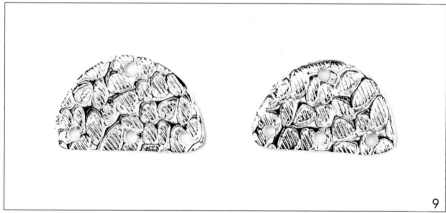

9

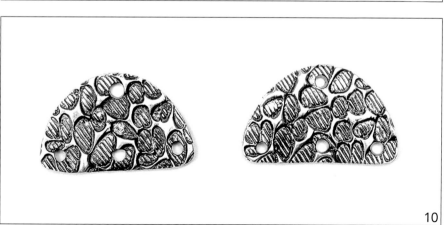

10

4 Carefully remove the imprinted piece of clay from the stamp (at this point your circle has become an oval).

5 Cut the oval into two equal halves with a tissue blade (a tissue blade works best for this type of project because it will not distort the shape of your pieces). Let the pieces dry completely.

6 File the pieces while holding them back to back so that the shapes remain identical.

7-8 Mark the location of the holes with a pencil **[7]**. (All holes should be approximately 2mm from the edge of the piece.) Place the tip of the scalpel or X-acto knife on top of one pencil mark. Hold the scalpel perpendicular to the piece and rotate the scalpel gently, without applying pressure **[8]**. Turn the piece over and repeat so that the hole is even on both sides. Continue until all of the holes have been carved out.

9-10 Fire the pieces according to the manufacturer's directions. Once the pieces are fired, polish them until the silver shines **[9]**. If you wish, use liver of sulfur to add a patina **[10]**.

- PMC3 clay
- **6** 24-gauge sterling silver head pins
- 18 in. (45.7cm) 22-gauge sterling silver round wire, half-hard
- sterling silver ear wires
- assorted 3–7mm beads
- unmounted rubber stamp mat
- round clay cutter, ¾ in. (1.9cm) diameter
- **10** playing cards
- roller
- plastic mat
- Badger Balm
- small brush
- cup of water
- paper towel
- flexible sanding pad
- X-acto knife or scalpel
- tissue blade
- roundnose pliers
- chainnose pliers
- side cutters
- pencil
- polishing pad
- liver of sulfur (optional)

Make the earrings

1 String five or six beads of your choice onto a head pin and make a wrapped loop (see p. 108) above the beads. Repeat with the five remaining head pins.

2 Cut a 3-in. (7.6cm) piece of 22-gauge wire and make the first half of a wrapped loop at one end. Slide the loop onto the loop of a head pin unit and finish the wraps.

3 String beads onto the wire and make the first half of a wrapped loop. Slide the loop into one of the three holes at the bottom of a textured earring component and finish the wraps.

4 Repeat steps 2–3 until you've made a dangle for each hole in the earring components. Attach an ear wire to the top of each earring component.

tip

These pieces are very versatile components. Try changing the number of holes and the orientation of the component for many different uses. For example, you can use two of these components as 3-to-1 components for a necklace or a bracelet (as in the Three-strand Garden Bracelet on p. 32), or make a single 2-to-1 component to create a "Y" necklace. See p. 40 for more ideas.

Charm Set

Create unique, sparkling jewelry components by setting a CZ in a ball of metal clay. This simple method is adaptable to any shape and size of stone, and the technique itself is adaptable as well. As you become more comfortable with it, you can experiment – cut and file the clay to create a bezel effect or use it in combination with other stone-setting methods and metal clay techniques.

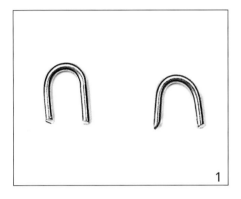

1

2

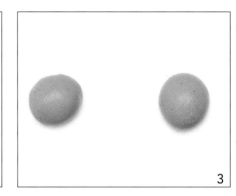

3

4

5

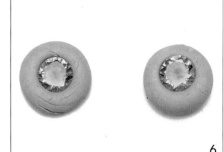

6

7

Make the earring components

1 Cut two 10mm lengths of 20-gauge fine silver wire and bend each piece into a U shape.

2-4 Cut two 2g (approximate) pieces of clay **[2]**. Roll each piece into a ball **[3]**, using liberal amounts of Badger Balm to assist the process. Flatten the balls slightly when finished **[4]**.

5-6 Use the tweezers to set a CZ on top of each piece of clay **[5]**, carefully pushing the CZs in until their edges sink below the line of clay **[6]**.

7 Using the tweezers, push a U-shaped wire into the edge of each clay piece. Let the pieces dry.

8 Once the pieces are dry, file them with the flexible sanding pad if necessary. If any cracks occur in the surface of the clay, fill the

tip

While you can use this technique by itself, this is also a good alternative to setting CZs using a syringe (especially if you're not entirely comfortable with syringe). See additional ideas on p. 41.

If you are using a CZ that is not round, shape the clay before pushing the CZ in. After it's dry, file to shape the sides to create a bezeled look. For more on filing to create a bezeled look, see the Twisted Lariat Ring, p. 58.

cracks with paste, dry the pieces, and file again.

9-10 Embellish the pieces with syringe [9]. It is a good idea to attach parts of the syringe to the U-shaped wire, giving it extra support [10]. Let the pieces dry, and file again if necessary.

11 Fire the pieces according to the manufacturer's directions. Polish the pieces until the silver shines.

Make the earrings

1 Cut a 3-in. (7.6cm) piece of 22-gauge wire and make the first half of a wrapped loop (see p. 108) at one end. Slide it through the U-shaped wire and finish the wraps.

2 String an assortment of beads and spacers on the wire. Make the first half of a wrapped loop above the beads, string an ear wire, and finish the wraps.

3 Repeat steps 1 and 2 to make the other earring.

Make the bracelet

1 My bracelet has six metal clay charms. To make these bracelet components, insert a second U-shaped wire directly opposite the first U-shaped wire. Embellish, fire, and polish the pieces as directed above.

materials

- PMC3 clay
- PMC3 syringe
- PMC3 paste
- 6mm kiln-ready CZs
- 20-gauge fine silver wire
- 27 in. (68.6cm) 22-gauge sterling silver round wire, half-hard
- 2-in. (5cm) 24-gauge sterling silver head pin
- sterling silver ear wires
- sterling silver toggle clasp
- sterling silver lobster claw clasp
- flexible beading wire
- **2** crimp beads
- sterling silver large-link chain
- assorted Austrian crystals and silver beads
- plastic mat
- small brush
- tweezers
- Badger Balm
- cup of water
- paper towel
- flexible sanding pads
- X-acto knife or scalpel
- chainnose pliers
- roundnose pliers
- side cutters
- crimping pliers

2 Cut a 2½-in. (6.4cm) piece of 22-gauge wire and make the first half of a wrapped loop on one end. String a silver spacer, a crystal, and a spacer, and make the first half of a wrapped loop after the beads. Repeat to make one more wrapped loop component than you have metal clay charms.

3 Attach one half of the clasp to one loop of a wrapped loop component, and finish the wraps. Attach a metal clay charm to the other loop of the wrapped loop component, and finish the wraps. Continue connecting the wrapped loop components to the metal clay charms. Finish by attaching the other half of the clasp to the last wrapped loop unit.

Make the necklace

1 To make the necklace components (my necklace has seven), insert a slightly narrower U-shaped wire perpendicular to the metal clay charm. Embellish, fire, and polish the pieces as directed above.

2 Center a metal clay charm on 20 in. (51cm) of flexible beading wire.

3 On one side, string a crystal, a silver bead, a crystal, and a metal clay charm. Repeat this pattern two more times.

4 String approximately 5 in. (12.7cm) of beads.

5 Repeat steps 3 and 4 on the other side of the wire, using the same bead sequence until reaching the desired length. My necklace is approximately 15 in. (38cm) long.

6 Crimp the lobster claw to one end of the necklace and the large-link chain to the other. Attach a silver head pin with an Austrian crystal to the end of the large link chain with a wrapped loop.

Jeweled Clasp

I constantly look for new ways to create unique jewelry components from metal clay – not just pendants and focal beads, but different types of findings, too. You'll be delighted by the possibilities of metal clay for creating custom components, including substantial, eye-catching clasps. This clasp, textured and then embellished with a CZ, easily serves as the focus of a piece.

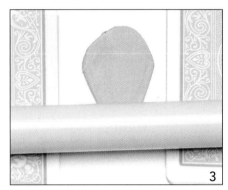

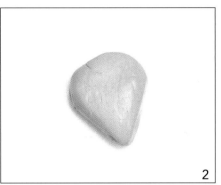

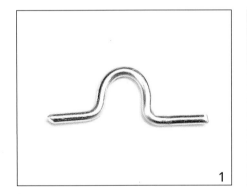

tip

It's best to use fine silver wire and findings in your metal clay pieces. Fine silver (as opposed to sterling silver) is 99.9% pure, just like metal clay, and won't develop fire scale during firing.

1 Make a 20–25mm wire shank from fine silver wire.

2-3 Cut approximately 4g of clay and smooth out the edges **[2]**, using Badger Balm liberally to prevent cracking. Roll the clay to the thickness of five cards **[3]**.

4-5 Apply extra Badger Balm to the side of the clay that will come in contact with the rubber stamp mat. Place the clay on the mat, oiled side down, and roll it to the thickness of four cards **[4]**. Carefully peel the clay off the rubber stamp mat and place it back on the plastic mat, textured side up **[5]**.

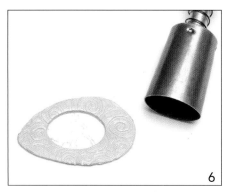

6

7

8

9

10

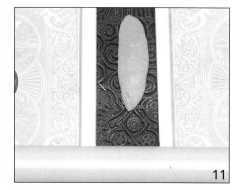

11

12

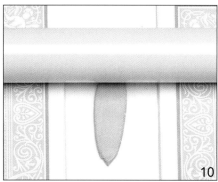

13

14

6 Use the clay cutter to punch out a shape in the center of the piece of clay. Remove the punched-out shape.

7 With a clean, slightly wet brush, shape and smooth the inside edge of the piece of clay. Let the piece dry.

8-9 Cut approximately 2 grams of clay to make the bar **[8]**. Smooth the edges and elongate the piece of clay, making one end more tapered than the other **[9]**.

10 Roll out the clay to the thickness of five cards, rolling it lengthwise so that it elongates even more.

tip

When you use a clay cutter to punch out an opening, dry the punched-out shape and save it for later use. These shapes make fun and versatile components for earrings, bracelets, etc. See p. 42 for more ideas.

11-12 Apply Badger Balm to one side of the clay, and place the clay, oiled side down, on the rubber stamp mat. Roll out the clay (again rolling it lengthwise) to the thickness of four cards **[11]**. Measure the clay, making sure the length of the bar is at least twice the width of the opening of the ring at its widest point. Peel the clay off the

15

mat and place it back on the plastic mat, textured side up. Let the piece dry **[12]**.

13-14 Once both pieces are dry, check the edges and file them if needed. Be sure to file the opening of the ring **[13]** as well as the edges of the pieces **[14]**.

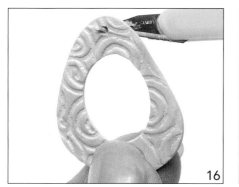

16

17

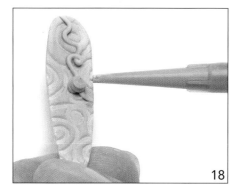

16

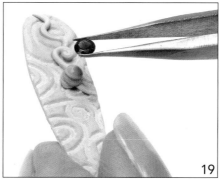

17

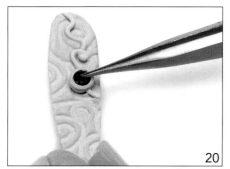

18

19

20

21

materials

- PMC3 clay
- PMC3 syringe
- PMC3 paste
- 18- or 20-gauge fine silver wire
- 3mm kiln-ready CZ or synthetic stone
- plastic mat
- Badger Balm
- roller
- small brush
- flexible sanding pads
- playing cards
- oval clay cutter
- tweezers
- polishing pad
- unmounted rubber stamp mat
- X-acto knife or scalpel
- cup of water
- paper towel
- pencil
- side cutters
- roundnose pliers
- chainnose or flatnose pliers
- liver of sulfur (optional)

15 Take the bar piece and turn it over so that the smooth side is up. Paint it liberally with thick paste and place the shank in the center of the bar. Let the shank dry, then apply one or two more coats of paste to reinforce the shank. Let the piece dry thoroughly.

16 Decide on the location for the hole on the ring piece, and mark it with a pencil. Place the tip of the X-acto knife on top of the mark carefully. Hold it at a right angle to the piece and gently rotate the knife without applying pressure. Turn the piece over and repeat so that the hole is even on both sides.

17 Embellish both pieces with syringe.

18-20 To set a CZ on the bar, wet the clay with your brush. With syringe, make a blob approximately the same size as or larger than the CZ you are about to set [18]. Using the tweezers, set the CZ on top of the blob [19] and carefully push it in, making sure the edge of the CZ is submerged [20] (see Setting a stone, p. 108). Let the embellished pieces dry thoroughly.

21 Fire the pieces according to the manufacturer's instructions. Polish them until the silver shines. If you wish, use liver of sulfur to add a patina.

Wire-wrapped
Cabochon Pendant

More ideas p. 43

This project combines metal clay with traditional wire wrapping. Here, I use a basic wire technique in a new way, to attach a cabochon to a base of textured metal clay.

Choose any stone that catches your eye. Since the cabochon is attached to the metal clay base after firing, you don't need to worry about choosing a stone that is kiln-safe.

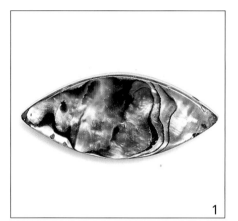
1

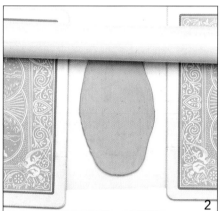
2

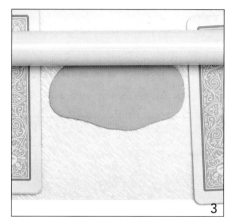
3

4

5

6

Make the metal clay component

1-2 Choose a cabochon (mine is approximately 35mm wide) **[1]**. Roll the clay out to the thickness of four cards, keeping in mind the size and shape of the cabochon and leaving a margin of clay accordingly **[2]**. If your plastic texture sheet is thicker or has a deep texture, it's best to use five cards.

3-4 Apply extra Badger Balm to one side of the rolled-out clay and place it on the texture sheet, oiled side down. Roll out the clay to the thickness of three cards **[3]**. Carefully remove the imprinted piece of clay from the texture sheet, and place it back on the plastic sheet, imprinted side up **[4]**.

5 Place the stone on top of the clay. Leaving at least a 5mm border of clay around the stone, use an X-acto knife or scalpel to cut out the desired outline. You can mirror the shape of the stone, as I did, or create a free-form design. When finished trimming the design, remove the cabochon and let the piece dry.

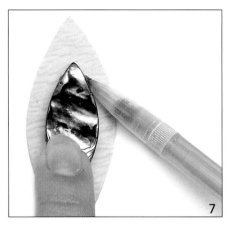

7

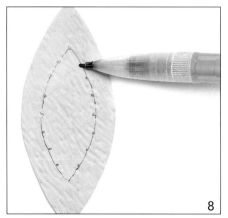

8

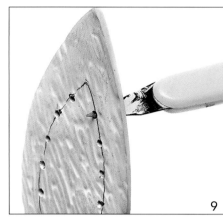

9

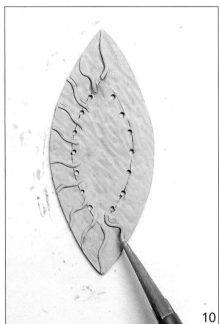

10

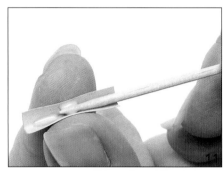

11

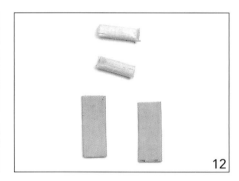

12

13

14

6 Sand the edges of the piece using a flexible sanding pad.

7-9 Place the cabochon back on the dried piece of clay and trace around it with a pencil [7]. Remove the cabochon, and use a pencil to mark the location of the holes, making them at least 3mm apart [8]. Place the tip of the X-acto knife carefully on top of a pencil mark [9]. Hold it at a right angle to the piece and gently rotate the knife without applying pressure. Turn the piece over and repeat so that the hole is even on both sides. Continue until all of the holes have been carved out.

10 Embellish your piece with syringe, making certain not to cover up the holes. Let it dry thoroughly.

11-14 To make the bails, cut a 10mm strip of sheet clay. Fold it in half lengthwise and glue it together with Elmer's glue [11]. Cut the strip into two 5mm strips. Cut two 5mm pieces of toothpick [12]. Glue the pieces of toothpick to the back of the pendant [13]. Glue the strips of sheet over the toothpicks and to the back of the pendant, making certain that the sheet does not extend over the top of the pendant [14]. Let the piece dry thoroughly.

15-16 Fire the piece according to the manufacturer's instructions, and polish the fired piece until the silver shines [15]. If you wish, use liver of sulfur to add a patina [16].

17 Place the stone on the front of the pendant, and begin wrapping it with wire by passing the 24-gauge wire from back to front through the holes. As you string the wire through the pendant to the front, add one or two beads per pass for extra embellishment. Conceal the wire ends by wrapping them around one of the wires holding the stone and then tucking them under the stone with your chainnose pliers.

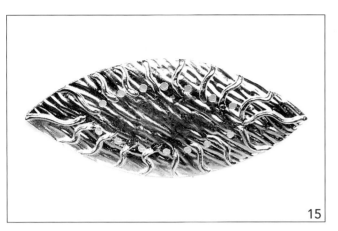

15

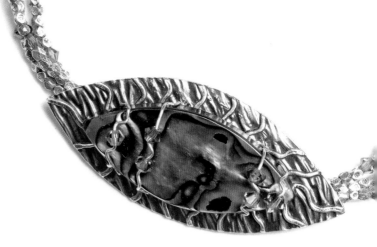

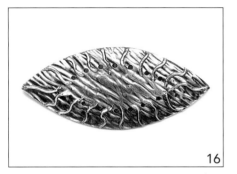

16

17

Tighten the wire wrap by holding the chainnose pliers perpendicular to the piece and gently bending each wire with the very tip of the pliers.

Make the necklace

1 Cut three 20-in. (51cm) pieces of flexible beading wire. String enough 2mm beads over all three wires to fill the gap between the two bails. String all three wires through each bail, and center the pendant on the wires. Separate the wires, and string assorted 2–3mm beads on each strand until you reach your desired necklace length.

2 Cut a 3-in. (7.6cm) piece of 22-gauge wire and make a wrapped loop at one end (see p. 108). String a crimp bead on one end of each strand of beading wire, and go through the wrapped loop with all three strands. Take each strand back through its crimp bead, crimp the crimp beads, and trim the excess wire. Repeat on the other

side of the necklace. String a cone and a bead on the 22-gauge wire on one side of the necklace, and make the first half of a wrapped loop. Attach the hook clasp to the loop and finish the wraps. Repeat on the other side of the necklace, attaching the wrapped loop to an end chain link.

3 String beads as desired on the three head pins and attach them to the end of the chain with wrapped loops.

tip

If you know ahead of time how you plan to wrap the stone, you can reduce the number of holes that you make in the piece.

materials

- PMC3 clay
- PMC3 syringe
- PMC+ sheet
- cabochon
- **3** 2-in. (5cm) 24-gauge sterling silver head pins
- 4–6 in. (10.2 x 15cm) 22-gauge sterling silver round wire, half-hard
- 24-gauge sterling silver round wire, dead soft
- flexible beading wire
- assorted 2–3mm beads
- **6** crimp beads
- **2** sterling silver cones
- sterling silver hook clasp
- 4 in. (10.2cm) sterling silver large-link chain
- texture sheet
- playing cards
- roller
- plastic mat
- small brush
- cup of water
- paper towel
- Badger Balm
- Elmer's glue
- sanding pad
- toothpick
- X-acto knife or scalpel
- pencil
- polishing pad
- roundnose pliers
- chainnose pliers
- side cutters
- crimping pliers
- liver of sulfur (optional)

Floral Cone Trio

I often turn to the natural world for inspiration and have experimented with using different types of seed pods to make jewelry components. Daylily pods, with graceful curves and a natural opening, are remarkably conducive to making cones. Their moderate size makes them suitable to stand alone as earrings, or to provide a unique finish for necklace and bracelet ends.

1

2

3

Make the floral cones

1 Choose pods, carefully considering their size and shape. Try to choose pods that are as similar as possible, since they will be used in pairs. The pods must be dry before you begin applying paste; if you're not certain whether a pod is completely dry, place it in a food dehydrator.

2-3 Leaving the pods on the stems, begin painting only the outside of each pod with paste [2]. Stop at the base of the stem. Let the first coat dry thoroughly, and begin applying the next coat. Each pod will need 8–10 coats of paste [3], and each coat must dry thoroughly before the next one is applied. Once the last coat of paste has been applied, let your pieces dry thoroughly.

tip

When you paint a pod or a leaf, it helps to keep the stem on in order to have something to hold. If the piece you've chosen does not have a stem, glue a toothpick to the base with Elmer's glue.

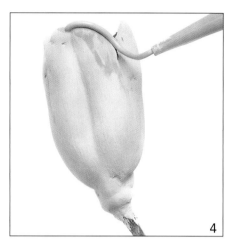
4

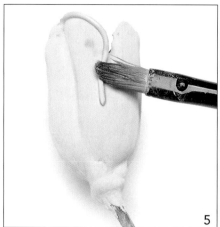
5

6

7

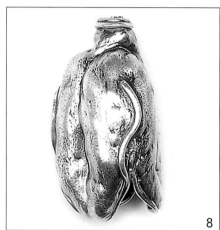
8

9

4-6 Use syringe to outline the edges of the pods **[4]**. Extend the syringe in the direction of the stem to add decorative touches, patting it down with a paintbrush to make sure it stays secure **[5]** (see p. 110 for more on syringe techniques). When finished outlining, use the syringe to create a spiral at the base of the stem where it meets the pod **[6]**. Let the pieces dry thoroughly. Once they dry, check the stems, and file away any extra clay on the stem with a metal file.

7-8 Fire the pieces according to the manufacturer's instructions, and polish the fired piece until the silver shines **[7]**. If you wish, use liver of sulfur to apply a patina **[8]**.

Make the earrings

1 String a 4mm round crystal on a head pin, and then a pod. String a 3mm bicone crystal and make a wrapped loop (see p. 108).

2 String a crystal on a piece of wire and make the first half of a wrapped loop at each end. Attach one end to the piece made in step 1, and attach the other end to an ear wire. Finish the wraps.

3 Repeat steps 1–2 to make the matching earring **[9]**.

Make the bracelet

1 Cut a 2½ in. (6.4cm) piece of wire and make a wrapped loop at one end. Repeat with another piece of wire.

2 Cut seven 10-in. (25.4cm) pieces of flexible beading wire. String a crimp bead on one strand, and go through the loop on one piece of wire. Go back through the crimp bead, and crimp the crimp bead. Repeat with the other six strands, attaching them to the same wire loop.

3 Determine the finished length of your bracelet, and subtract the combined length of the pods and clasp. String an assortment of 2–5mm beads onto each strand to this length. Use mostly smaller beads for the last ½ in. (1.3cm) on each side.

4 String a crimp bead on one strand, go through the wrapped loop on the remaining wire, and go back through the crimp bead. Crimp the crimp bead. Repeat with the other six strands, attaching them to the same loop.

5 String a pod cone over one wire so that it covers the wrapped loop and the end of the beaded strands. String a crystal on the wire, and make the first half of a wrapped loop. Slide one half of the clasp onto the loop and finish the wraps. Repeat at the other end.

6 Begin a wrapped loop, and string all seven strands onto it. Finish the loop and string a pod cone over it. String a crystal above the pod cone, and begin a wrapped loop. String one part of the toggle clasp onto the loop, and finish wrapping. Repeat for the other side.

Make the necklace

1 Cut a 2½ in. (6.4cm) piece of wire, and make a wrapped loop at one end. Repeat with another piece of wire.

2 Cut nine 10-in. (25.4cm) pieces of flexible beading wire. String a crimp bead on one strand, and go through the loop on one piece of wire. Go back through the crimp bead, and crimp the crimp bead. Repeat with the other eight strands, attaching them to the same wire loop.

3 String an assortment of beads onto each strand, using mostly smaller beads for the last ½ in. (1.3cm) on each side. Crimp each strand, making sure they are all the same length, approximately 5½ in. long.

4 String a crimp bead on one strand, go through the wrapped loop on the remaining wire, and go back through the crimp bead. Crimp the crimp bead. Repeat with the other eight strands, attaching them to the same loop.

5 String a pod cone over one wire so that it covers the wrapped loop and the end of the beaded strands. String a crystal on the wire and make the first half of a wrapped loop.

6 Cut two 8-in. (20.3cm) pieces of flexible beading wire. String one onto a wrapped loop above a pod cone, string a crimp bead, and crimp the crimp bead. String approximately 4 in. of beads, then string a crimp bead and the hook clasp. Crimp the crimp bead. Repeat on the other side of the necklace, finishing with the large-link chain instead of the clasp.

7 String a crystal on a head pin and use a wrapped loop to attach it to the free end of the large-link chain.

materials

- PMC3 paste
- PMC3 syringe
- assorted 2–5mm Austrian crystals, CZs, and silver beads
- 22-gauge sterling silver round wire, half-hard
- **3** 24-gauge sterling silver head pins
- sterling silver ear wires
- flexible beading wire
- sterling silver large-link chain
- crimp beads
- sterling silver toggle clasp
- sterling silver hook clasp
- daylily pods
- small brush
- cup of water
- paper towel
- metal file
- polishing pad
- roundnose pliers
- chainnose pliers
- crimping pliers
- side cutters
- liver of sulfur (optional)

Riveted Bead

Lampwork and fused art beads are available in a dazzling array of colors, and I often picture them accented by silver. PMC3 and other low-fire metal clays allow glass to be fired with the metal clay, making it possible to add bead caps, spirals, and other embellishments to art glass beads.

Choose a beautiful bead and enhance its beauty with metal clay, creating a truly memorable mixed-media piece.

Make the metal clay bead caps

1-2 With a small brush, paint a layer of paste on the inside of the hole of the bead **[1]**. Let the paste dry thoroughly, and apply another layer **[2]**.

3 Roll the clay out to the thickness of four cards.

4 Apply extra Badger Balm to one side of the rolled-out clay and place it on the rubber stamp mat, oiled side down. Roll the clay out again to the thickness of three cards, and carefully remove the imprinted clay from the stamp.

5-6 Use a round clay cutter to punch out a circle **[5]**.

tip

The bead shown here measures 15mm, so I used a ½-in. (1.3cm) round clay cutter and a ¼-in. (6mm) square cutter to make the caps. Choose your cutters according to the size of your bead.

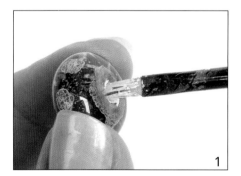

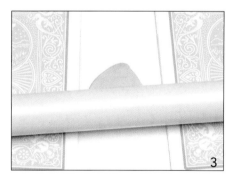

1

2

3

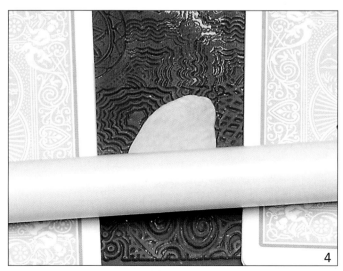

4

5

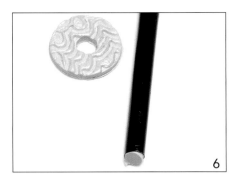

6

7

8

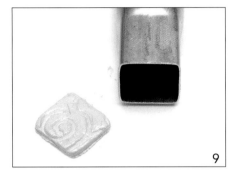

9

10

11

materials

- PMC3 clay
- PMC3 syringe
- PMC3 paste
- lampwork bead with a large hole (bead shown here by Jeff Plath)
- flexible beading wire
- assorted 2–4mm beads
- 4 in. (10.2cm) sterling silver large-link chain
- 2-in. (5cm) 24-gauge sterling silver head pin
- sterling silver hook clasp
- **2** crimp beads
- unmounted rubber stamp mat
- round clay cutter
- square clay cutter
- playing cards
- roller
- plastic mat
- Badger Balm
- small brush
- cup of water
- paper towel
- cocktail straw
- X-acto knife or scalpel
- crimping pliers
- side cutters
- roundnose pliers
- chainnose pliers

Remove the circle, place it on the plastic mat, and use a cocktail straw to punch a hole in the center of the circle **[6]**.

7-8 Place the "cap" on the bead **[7]**. Use syringe around the edge of the cap **[8]**, making certain to pat it with your brush to make it adhere.

9-10 Repeat steps 3–6 using a square punch instead of a round punch **[9, 10]**.

11-12 Attach the square cap to the round cap with paste or syringe **[11]**. If any paste or syringe oozes out the seams, be sure to clean it up with a clean, slightly wet brush. Let the piece dry. Once dry, check the bead to see if any metal clay has dried onto the glass below the cap. If it has, gently scrape the dried clay off with a scalpel or X-acto knife **[12]**.

13 Repeat steps 2–12 on the other side of the bead. Fire the piece at a temperature not higher than 1300°F (704°C). Be sure to let the kiln cool gradually, and do not open the kiln door until the kiln has cooled. Do not crash cool your piece by dipping it in water or placing it on a cold surface. (An abrupt change in temperature can cause the lampwork bead to crack.) Once the piece has cooled, polish it until the silver shines.

12

13

tip

If you do not have clay cutters in suitable shapes and sizes, cut shapes out of paper, place them on top of the clay, and carefully cut around the shapes with a scalpel or X-acto knife.

Make the necklace

1 Center the riveted bead on a 20-in. (51cm) length of flexible beading wire.

2 String an assortment of beads on each side of the bead until you reach the desired length.

3 On one end, string a crimp bead and the hook clasp. Go back through the crimp bead and a few more beads, and crimp the crimp bead. Trim the excess wire. Repeat on the other end, stringing an end of large-link chain instead of the clasp. Go back through the crimp bead, crimp, and trim the excess wire.

4 String a bead on a head pin, and make the first half of a wrapped loop above the bead. Attach the loop to the free end of the chain and finish the wraps.

Three-strand Garden Bracelet

Some metal clay jewelry components stand alone, while others work seamlessly together to create a beautiful finished piece of jewelry. Here, toothpicks and metal clay slip are used to make channels on the back of individual bracelet links, turning them into three-strand components.

I like to use organic elements in my designs, so tiny leaves embellish these components. The leaves are simple and fun to make, and the pinched ends of each leaf offer beginners a bit of hands-on metal clay work.

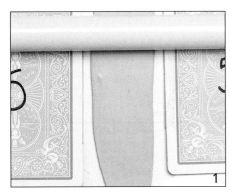

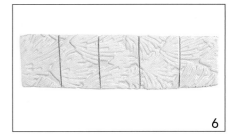

Make the bracelet links

Cut two strips of paper: one for the bracelet length, the other for the link width. Keep in mind that the clay will shrink by approximately 10% during firing. If the strip of paper determining the length is 20mm pre-firing, the fired piece will measure 18mm. My finished bracelet includes five components, each measuring 15 x 20mm.

1-3 Shape the clay into a square with your fingers. Roll the clay out to the thickness of five cards, rolling it in one direction and elongating it [1]. Keep in mind the

dimensions of the components as you roll. Apply extra Badger Balm to one side of the rolled-out clay and place it on the texture sheet, oiled side down. Roll the clay out again to the thickness of three cards [2]. Carefully remove the imprinted piece of clay from the texture sheet and place the clay back on the plastic mat, imprinted side up [3].

4-6 Using the paper strips for measurements, use an X-acto knife or scalpel to trim the clay lengthwise [4] and cut out individual components [5]. Let the pieces dry [6].

7 Use your sanding pad or emery board to file the edges of each piece, making sure that the pieces stay relatively uniform in size.

8 With a pencil, mark three parallel lines on the back of each piece (the positioning of lines on each piece should be the same).

9 Cut toothpicks into segments equal in width to the clay components. Glue three toothpick segments to the back of each component, matching them to the pencil marks.

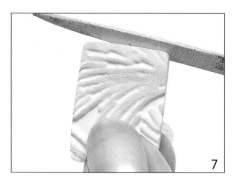

7

8

9

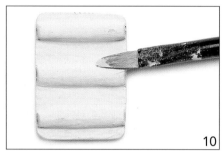

10

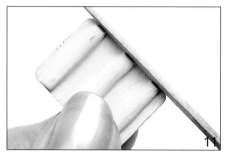

11

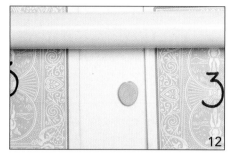

12

13

14

15

10 Paint the back of each component, including the toothpick pieces, with eight to ten layers of paste, letting the paste dry completely between coats.

11 File the edges of the components, making sure there is no clay over the ends of the toothpicks.

12-16 Make small leaf embellishments for your bracelet components. First, roll out small pieces of clay (approximately 1g each) to the thickness of three cards **[12]**. Place a leaf, vein side down, over the clay, and roll the clay out again **[13]**. Remove the imprinted clay from the leaf and cut out a leaf shape outline with the X-acto knife or scalpel **[14]**. Pinch the base of the leaf shape with your fingers **[15]**. Repeat four more times to make a leaf for each bracelet component. If you wish, you can make more and attach multiple leaf embellishments to some components. Let the pieces dry, then file the edges **[16]**.

17-21 Attach the leaf components to the imprinted sides of the components with syringe **[17]** or paste **[18–20]**. Remove any excess syringe or paste with a clean, slightly wet brush. Let the pieces dry **[21]**.

22 Make two 3-to-1 components from the Textured Earrings project (see p. 8). Make sure the holes line up with the toothpicks on the back of each bracelet component.

23 Fire all of the components according to the manufacturer's instructions. Once fired, polish them until the silver shines. If you wish, use liver of sulfur to add a patina.

Make the bracelet

1 Cut a 3-in. (7.6cm) piece of 22-gauge wire and make the first half of a wrapped loop at one end. Attach the loop to the loop of a toggle clasp and finish the wraps.

2 String a crystal on the wire, and make the first half of a wrapped loop. Attach the loop to the single hole of a 3-to-1 connector and finish the wraps.

3 Repeat steps 1 and 2 with the other clasp half and 3-to-1 connector.

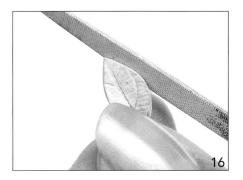

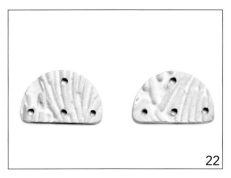

materials

- PMC3 clay
- PMC3 syringe
- PMC3 paste
- 22-gauge sterling silver round wire, half-hard
- sterling silver toggle clasp
- flexible beading wire, size .014
- 6 crimp beads
- assorted 2–4mm beads
- small leaf with well-defined veins
- texture sheet
- playing cards
- roller
- plastic mat
- Badger Balm
- small brush
- cup of water
- paper towel
- paper
- flexible sanding pad or emery board
- files
- X-acto knife or scalpel
- toothpicks
- pencil
- polishing pad
- roundnose pliers
- chainnose pliers
- side cutters
- crimping pliers
- liver of sulfur (optional)

4 Cut three 9-in. (23cm) strands of flexible beading wire. On one end of a wire, string a crimp bead, and go through one of the three holes on the connector. Go back through the crimp bead, and crimp the crimp bead. Repeat with the other two wires.

5 On each strand, string a crystal, a spacer, and a crystal, and one hole of a bracelet link. Repeat until all the links have been strung and the bracelet is the desired length.

6 String a crimp bead on each wire, go through the correspond-ing holes in the remaining 3-to-1 connector, and go back through the crimp beads plus a few more beads on each strand. Crimp the crimp beads and trim the excess wire.

tip

Rather than let leftover clay bits go to waste, I often make tiny leaf components, since clay is best used when fresh. I let them dry, and then I use them whenever I need a little organic embellishment.

Bezel-set Gem Pendant

Many pieces of metal clay jewelry focus on the clay and use small CZs as embellishments. This piece is different; it uses sheet clay and a small amount of syringe to create a setting for a stunning trillion CZ. The sheet clay makes a crisp, clean setting reminiscent of traditional metalsmithing bezel techniques.

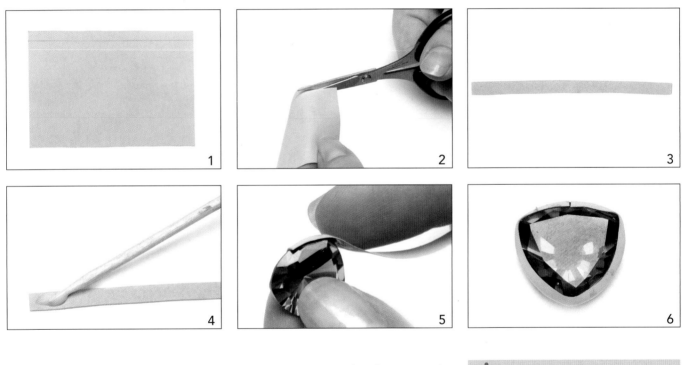

1-3 Use a pencil to gently mark a piece of PMC sheet 4mm wide [1]. Use small, sharp scissors to cut it [2, 3].

4-6 Use a toothpick to spread glue along the length of the strip [4] and glue the strip all the way around the edge of the CZ, beginning and ending the strip where you plan to place the bail [5]. Trim any excess strip [6].

tip

For a classic look, laminate two to three layers of sheet to use as the bezel instead of a single layer and eliminate the syringe. See additional bezeling ideas on p. 47.

7

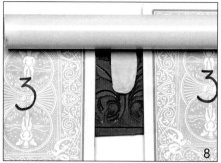

8

9

10

11

12

13

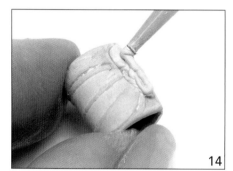

14

15

materials

- PMC3 clay
- PMC3 syringe
- PMC+ sheet
- large (16 x 16mm) trillion CZ
- casting grain
- playing cards
- roller
- plastic mat
- unmounted rubber stamp mat
- small brush
- cup of water
- paper towel
- tweezers
- straw
- Elmer's glue
- Badger Balm
- flexible sanding pad
- metal files
- X-acto knife or scalpel

7-12 To make the bail, roll the clay out to the thickness of four cards [7]. Your piece should be about 10–12mm wide. Apply extra Badger Balm to one side of the rolled-out clay and place it on the rubber stamp mat, oiled side down. Roll it out again to the thickness of three cards [8]. Carefully remove the imprinted piece of clay from the stamp, and trim the long edges with a scalpel or X-acto knife [9]. Wrap the trimmed piece around a well-greased straw, using syringe clay to adhere the two edges together [10, 11]. Trim the excess clay at the base of the straw [12], and fill the seam with syringe. Let the bail dry.

13-16 When the bail has dried, file any sharp edges [13] and then use syringe to attach the bail to the bezeled CZ [14, 15]. Use a brush to remove any excess syringe. Let the piece dry [16].

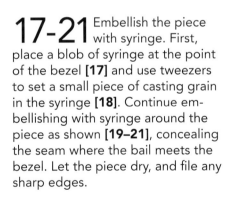

17-21 Embellish the piece with syringe. First, place a blob of syringe at the point of the bezel **[17]** and use tweezers to set a small piece of casting grain in the syringe **[18]**. Continue embellishing with syringe around the piece as shown **[19–21]**, concealing the seam where the bail meets the bezel. Let the piece dry, and file any sharp edges.

22 Fire according to the manufacturer's instructions for PMC+. To avoid cracking the CZ, be sure to let the kiln cool gradually: Do not open the kiln door until the kiln is cool, and do not crash cool your piece. Polish the fired piece until the silver shines. If you wish, use liver of sulfur to add a patina.

Create a whole wardrobe of simple, fun earrings by varying the texture and shape used.

More *Textured Earring* ideas

Make a textured 2-to-1 component the centerpiece of a Y necklace.

The earring component becomes a 3-to-1 connector in this necklace. Here I used a leaf imprint instead of a texture sheet.

Before setting the stone, stamp the ball of clay.

More *Charm Set* ideas

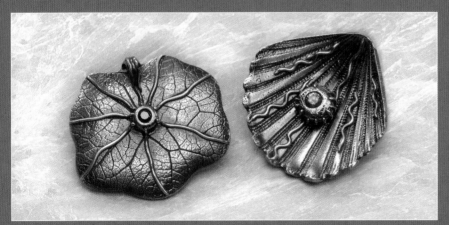

Create pendants that combine the charm technique with others, such as leaf imprinting or using a seashell as a mold (see p. 86).

More *Jeweled Clasp* ideas

A rubber stamp is an interesting alternative to a texture sheet for imprinting the pieces.

Imprint a leaf and embellish the pieces with syringe.

Save the punched-out shapes from a project like the jeweled clasp and use them to make earring and bracelet components.

This set is formed from a coil of clay that I arranged in graceful curves.

Different shapes and sizes of cabochons suggest a variety of base shapes. Use this technique to create pendants, brooches, and earrings.

This pendant was made from a peony pod.

More *Floral Cone* ideas

A magnolia pod became a vessel.

A wild garlic pod made a beautiful pendant.

I formed this pendant around a lily pod. When you're out in nature, keep your eyes open and look around you; part of the fun is discovering natural forms that you can use in your designs.

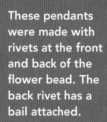

These pendants were made with rivets at the front and back of the flower bead. The back rivet has a bail attached.

Flower beads by Nanette Young-Grenier

Add leaves and other small embellishments to the rivets.

Create rivets that follow the shape of the bead.

Consider making tapered components for a necklace using the technique you learned making the Garden Bracelet. These components are embellished with tiny leaves like those on the bracelet links. Use just the leaves for small, simple earrings.

More *Garden Components* ideas

The same technique, using toothpicks and layers of paste, created two channels on the back of this leaf pendant for a double-strand necklace.

The bezeling technique combines with a shell mold in this pendant.

An imprinted leaf embellishes the bottom of this bezel setting.

If you laminate the metal clay sheet (use a double thickness), it is not necessary to reinforce it with syringe. You can embellish the bezel with leaves, as I did on the red necklace and earring set.

Intermediate
Projects

Artists with some metal clay experience will find these ten projects perfectly suited to their level. Beginners who have worked their way through the first eight projects, gradually building their skill level, also will find they have the background to complete these intermediate projects with great success. As in the first section, each project introduces a new way of working with the metal clay, so that by the time you finish the book, you will have an impressive repertoire of metal clay techniques to call your own.

The projects that follow include a range of organic-themed adornments, including rings, pendants, beads, brooches, and more. For more ideas that will stretch your creativity, enjoy the Inspiration Gallery that begins on p. 90.

Garden Ring Trio

More ideas p. 90

Of all the projects I teach in my metal clay classes, these garden rings and their variations consistently have been the most popular.

These rings are very versatile. Embellish yours with tiny leaves and casting grain, syringe clay and sparkling CZs, or pearls, crystals, and wire.

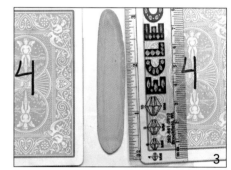

Make the basic garden ring

1 Wrap the piece of paper or Post-It around the mandrel at the size marking that is two sizes larger than your ring's finished size. Wind transparent tape around the paper until the entire piece is covered. Grease the tape liberally.

2 Shape the clay into a long cylinder with your fingers.

3 Roll the clay to the thickness of four cards. For most sizes, 3 in. (7.6cm) long will be sufficient.

4-6 Place the leaf on top of the clay and roll over it again, imprinting the leaf into the clay **[4]**. Remove the leaf **[5]** and cut out the shape of the band using a tissue blade or a scalpel **[6]**.

7-8 Wrap the clay strip around the mandrel **[7]**. Connect the two sides of the strip with syringe, trimming any excess clay away with the scalpel **[8]**. With a clean, slightly wet brush, push the two sides of the ring together to make them adhere. Place the mandrel on the rests and let the piece dry.

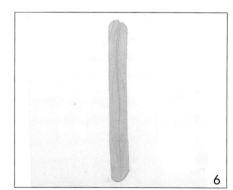

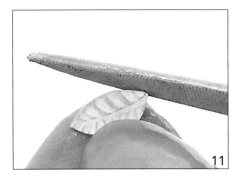

materials

9 When the ring is dry, take it off the mandrel and remove the piece of paper. If the two sides of the band pull apart, repair with syringe and be certain to fill in the seam from the inside. Dry your piece again, and use flexible sanding pads and metal files to file the ring so that there are no sharp edges. Pay particular attention to the inside of the ring, making it as smooth as possible.

10-11 Make small leaves to use as embellishment. You can use the scraps of clay left over from trimming the ring band, or you can roll out another piece of clay to the thickness of three cards. Apply extra Badger Balm to one side of the clay. Push the clay into the vintage stamp to imprint it. Cut out the leaves **[10]**, dry them, and shape them by filing with a metal file **[11]**.

12 Attach the leaves to the ring with syringe.

13-14 Embellish the ring with syringe, at the same time taking care to conceal the seam **[13, 14]**. Let the piece dry and file if needed.

15 Fire according to the manufacturer's instructions. If you wish, use a HattieS Pattie to support the ring during firing. After firing, remove the HattieS Pattie according to the manufacturer's instructions. Polish the fired piece until the silver shines. If you wish, use liver of sulfur to apply a patina.

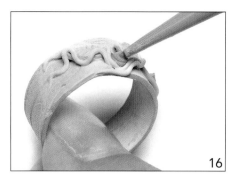

16

17

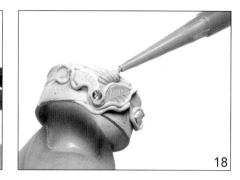

18

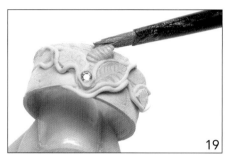

19

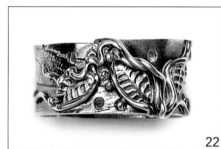

20

tip

Rings are subject to more stress and wear than most other jewelry. Because of this, I recommend that you fire them at the maximum temperature (1650°F/900°C) and length of time (two hours) for the most shrinkage, density, and durability.

21

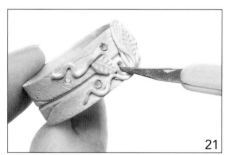

22

Make a garden ring with CZs

1 Follow steps 1 through 14 for the basic garden ring.

2 Create syringe blobs similar in size and shape to the CZs you are about to set, and shape them with a clean, slightly wet brush **[16–20]**. Push the CZs in.

3 Follow step 15 of the garden ring.

Make a beaded garden ring

1 Follow steps 1 through 14 for the basic garden ring.

2 Mark the locations for the holes with a pencil, placing the holes at least 2mm from the edge of the band. To carve the holes, place the tip of the X-acto knife or scalpel on the pencil mark. Hold it at a right angle to the piece and rotate the knife gently without applying pressure **[21]**. Continue until all of the holes have been carved out.

3 Follow step 15 of the garden ring **[22]**.

4 Embellish the ring with wire and beads, lacing the wire through the holes and concealing the ends of the wire by wrapping them around the wires on the outside of the ring or making wire spirals.

Porcelain Fairy Pendant

The earth tones and natural themes of many porcelain cabochons combine well with the organic elements I like to use in my metal clay jewelry. Thanks to low-fire metal clay, glazed porcelain can be incorporated into metal clay pieces and fired in the kiln. Here, a lovely fairy face is placed on an imprinted leaf and embellished with syringe "hair," creating a whimsical pendant.

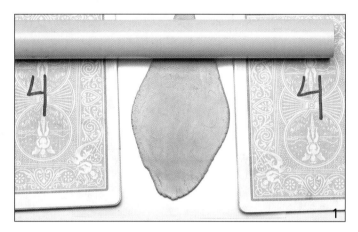

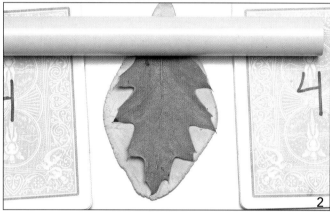

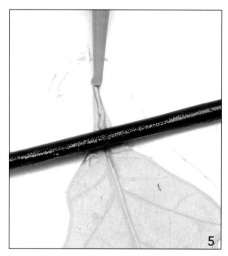

tip

Although porcelain can withstand low-fire metal clay temperatures, not all glazes can. If you wish, test-fire a sample cabochon by itself, using the temperature at which you plan to fire the finished piece.

1 Roll the clay out to the thickness of four cards. Be sure to roll the clay out so it will accommodate the leaf, leaving an additional 15mm of clay where the bail will be located.

2-4 Remove the stem of the leaf. Place the leaf on the clay, vein side down, and roll over to imprint it into the clay **[2]**, making sure that your roller rests on the card stacks at all times. Carefully remove the leaf **[3]**. Use tweezers if necessary. Trim the excess clay around the leaf image, leaving a tapered wedge at least 15mm long for the bail **[4]**.

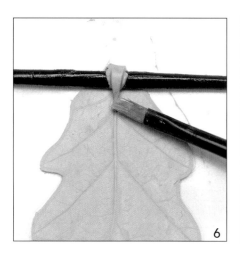

6

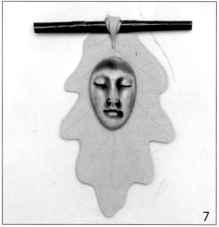

7

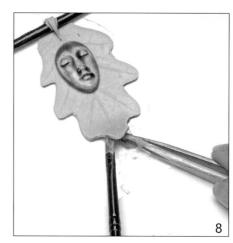

8

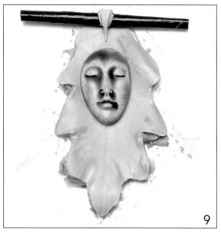

9

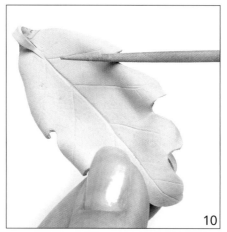

10

11

materials

- PMC3 clay
- PMC3 syringe
- PMC3 paste
- porcelain fairy cabochon (by Melanie Brooks)
- large leaf with well-defined veins
- playing cards
- roller
- plastic mat
- Badger Balm
- small brush
- tweezers
- cocktail straw
- cup of water
- paper towel
- metal file
- tissue paper
- flexible sanding pad
- X-acto knife or scalpel
- vermiculite
- polishing pad
- liver of sulfur (optional)

5-6 To make the bail, grease the straw liberally. Place the straw at the base of the wedge that is intended for the bail **[5]**. Experimentally roll the bail over until you have the best possible placement. Put a drop of syringe on the underside of the tip of the wedge. Roll the wedge over to create the bail. Use a brush to gently press the tip of the bail into place **[6]**. Don't use your fingertip because it will leave an imprint.

7-9 Decide where the cabochon is going to be placed on the leaf **[7]**. Ball up small pieces of tissue paper and carefully slip them under portions of the leaf while lifting up the clay with the brush **[8]**. Once the tissue paper is in place, gently shape the clay with the brush **[9]**. Let the piece dry.

10-11 Use metal files **[10]** and a flexible sanding pad **[11]** to file the edges, bail, and back so there are no sharp edges.

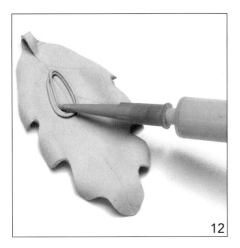

12

13

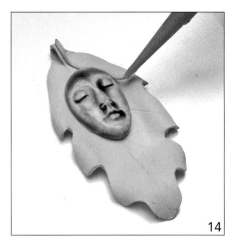

14

15

16

tip

Use a larger leaf just as you would a texture sheet. If the shape you want is unavailable, imprint a larger leaf and then cut out the shape afterward. For example, if you would like to create a piece with an oak leaf design, but an oak leaf is unavailable, you can use a large maple leaf to imprint the clay, and then cut out the shape of an oak leaf.

12-13 Brush the entire leaf with water. Use syringe or paste (I used syringe) to attach the cabochon to the leaf [**12, 13**].

14-15 Start embellishing with your syringe at the top of the bail, continuing the syringe onto the cabochon to make the "hair" [**14**]. Zigzag between the cabochon and the leaf with the syringe trail, being sure to attach the cabochon to the leaf with the syringe "hair" [**15**]. Repeat this two to three times per side, creating a syringe bezel around the cabochon. Let the piece dry.

16 Fire the piece in vermiculite to support the shape of the leaf. Be sure to let the kiln cool gradually. Do not open the kiln door or crash cool your piece. Polish the fired piece until the silver shines. If you wish, use liver of sulfur to apply a patina.

Twisted Lariat Ring

More ideas p. 92

This versatile necklace features an unusual twisted, textured lariat ring. One of the strengths of this piece is that you can incorporate different design elements such as color and texture to complement the beads used in the necklace, creating a more cohesive look.

Make the lariat ring

1 Shape approximately 16g of clay into a cylinder.

2 With the coil roller, roll the clay until it is approximately 4½ in. (11.4cm) long with tapered ends.

3-5 Apply Badger Balm to the coil and place it on the rubber stamp mat. Place the lace on top of the coil **[3]**. Gently roll it out again the long way to slightly flatten it **[4]**. It should now measure 5–5½ in. (12.7–14cm) long. Carefully remove the coil from the stamp. Trim the

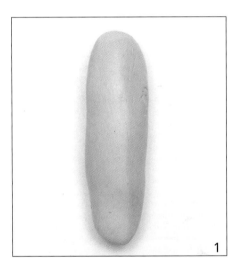

1

2

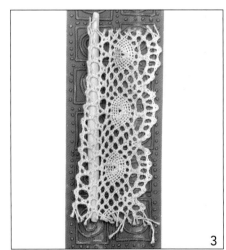

3

4

5

6

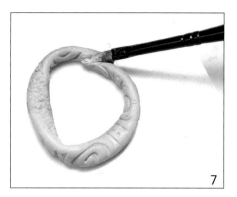

7

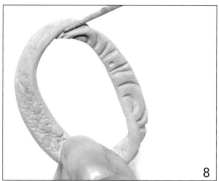

8

9

10

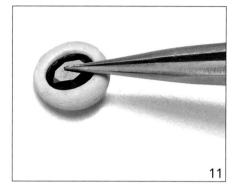

11

12

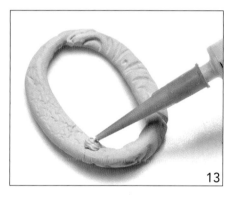

13

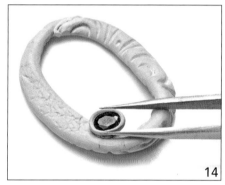

14

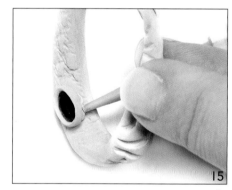

15

ends with a scalpel to further taper the ends **[5]**.

6-7 Twist the coil 360° and bring the tapered ends together to make a ring. Overlap the ends. Join the ends with syringe **[6]**, blending the syringe seam with a brush **[7]**. Let the piece dry.

8 Sand your piece with a flexible sanding pad. Smooth the seam where the ends meet with a metal file.

9 Embellish your piece with syringe on both sides, at the same time concealing the seam.

10-16 To set the large CZ, roll a piece of clay into a ball (using liberal amounts of Badger Balm helps) **[10]**. Make it slightly elongated. Push the CZ into the clay until the edge or girdle of the CZ sinks below the line of clay **[11]** (see Setting a stone, p. 108). Let it dry and file away any sharp edges. Continue filing to give the clay a bezeled appearance **[12]**. Moisten the bezeled CZ component and the ring. Attach the component to the

ring using syringe **[13–15]**. Let the piece dry and file away any sharp edges **[16]**.

17-19 To set the three smaller CZs on the other side, moisten the clay with your brush. With syringe, make a blob for each CZ approximately the size of the CZ you are about to set (or larger) **[17]**. Using tweezers, set a CZ on top of each blob and carefully push it in **[18]**, making sure the girdle is below the line of clay. Let the piece dry **[19]**.

20-21 Fire the piece according to the manufacturer's instructions and polish until the silver shines **[20]**. If you wish, use liver of sulfur to apply a patina **[21]**.

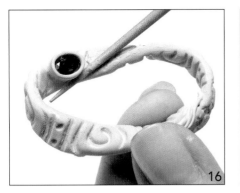

16

17

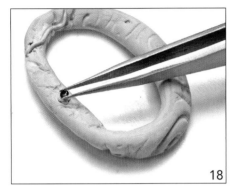

16

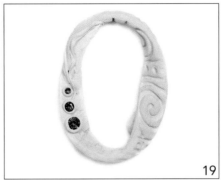

17

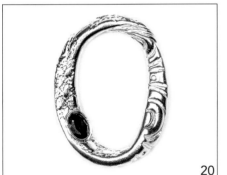

18

19

20

21

materials

- PMC3 clay
- PMC3 syringe
- 24-gauge sterling silver head pins
- **2** 1-in. (2.5cm) lengths sterling silver large-link chain
- flexible beading wire
- **2** crimp beads
- CZs
- assorted beads, 2–12mm
- unmounted rubber stamp mat
- lace
- roller
- coil roller
- plastic mat
- Badger Balm
- small brush
- cup of water
- paper towel
- flexible sanding pad
- tweezers
- X-acto knife or scalpel
- roundnose pliers
- chainnose pliers
- side cutters
- crimping pliers
- polishing pad
- liver of sulfur (optional)

Make the necklace

1 Cut 60 in. (1.5m) of flexible beading wire. Determine how many 2mm beads are needed to make a bail for the lariat ring, and center that number of beads on the wire. Wrap the beading wire around the ring, and adjust the wire ends so one is 1 in. (2.5cm) shorter than the other. String both pieces of wire through one bead, separate the strands, and string an assortment of beads on each strand until the desired length is reached. String a crimp bead on one wire end, and string an end link of chain. Go back through the crimp bead and a few more beads, crimp the crimp bead, and trim the excess wire. Repeat with the other wire end.

2 String beads on head pins as desired, and make the first half of a wrapped loop above each. Attach each head pin to the chain links and finish the wraps.

Mermaid's Necklace

More ideas p. 93

Many of my projects incorporate seed pods, leaves, and flowers, but I also find inspiration in another part of the natural world: the ocean. Seashells are beautiful, and they come in a multitude of shapes, textures, and sizes that are perfect for creating necklace, bracelet, and earring components.

I chose a half-drilled pearl to complement this seashell. The natural material highlights the shape and texture of the shell, and the half-drilled pearl, more of a gem than a bead, adds grace and elegance.

Make the pendant

Choose a slightly concave shell with interesting textures, such as a scallop shell.

1 Roll the clay out to the thickness of five cards, making certain that the rolled-out piece of clay will accommodate the shape and size of the shell.

2-5 Apply Badger Balm to one side of the rolled-out clay and place it on the shell, oiled side down [2]. Gently work the clay onto the shell with your fingers. Then, use

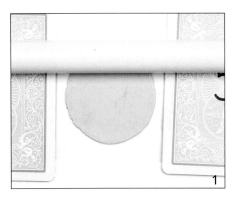

7

8

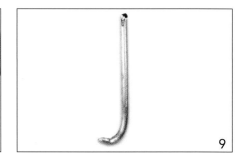
9

10

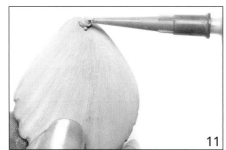
11

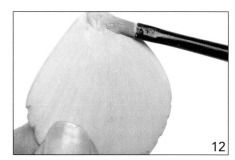
12

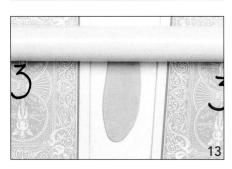
13

14

15

the brush in the same manner, moving in the direction of the ridges **[3]**. Trim the excess clay with the X-acto knife **[4, 5]**. Let the piece dry.

6-7 Carefully remove the clay from the shell. File between the ridges with a round metal file **[6]** and sand with a flexible sanding pad **[7]**.

8 Create a hole at the tip of the shell by placing the tip of the X-acto knife approximately 3–4mm below the tip of the shell. Hold it at a right angle to the piece and gently rotate the knife without applying pressure. Then turn the piece over and repeat so that the hole is even on both sides.

9-12 Using the chainnose pliers, create an L-shaped component with the fine silver wire **[9]**. String the wire L through the hole in the shell piece so the long wire ends up on the concave side

of the shell **[10]**. Use the syringe to make a large blob to secure the L at the reverse of the shell **[11]**. Use the brush to smooth the clay **[12]**. Let the piece dry.

13-17 To make the bail, roll a piece of clay, approximately 15 x 5mm, to the thickness of three cards **[13]**. Trim the edges to make a rectangle **[14]**. Wrap the clay around a well-greased straw. Connect the two ends with syringe **[15]** and pinch the bail closed **[16]**. Let it dry. Once dry, file away any sharp edges **[17]**.

18-19 Use syringe to attach the bail to the back of the piece, concealing the section of clay holding the L component **[18]**. Smooth out the excess with a brush **[19]**. Let the piece dry.

20-23 Fire according to the manufacturer's instructions. Polish the fired piece until

the silver shines **[20]**. If you wish, use liver of sulfur to add a patina **[21]**. If needed, trim the L-shaped wire **[22]**. Use two-part epoxy to attach the pearl **[23]**.

Make the necklace

1 Center the pendant on two silk strands and three 20-in. (51cm) pieces of flexible beading wire.

2 Determine the desired length of the necklace, and subtract the length of the clasp.

3 String the three strands of flexible beading wire with an assortment of seed beads, pearls, and Austrian crystals until you've reached the length determined in step 2.

4 Cut a 3-in. (7.6cm) piece of 22-gauge wire and make the first half of a wrapped loop. Pierce the two silk strands at the desired length

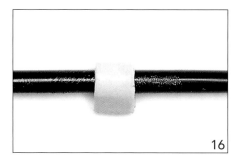

16

17

18

19

20

21

22

23

and finish the wraps. String a crimp bead on each strand of beading wire. Take all three strands through the wrapped loop and back through the crimp bead and a few more beads on each strand, and crimp the crimp beads. Trim the silk ends, string a cone and a bead on the wire, and make the first half of a wrapped loop above the bead. Slide the S-hook onto the wire and finish the wraps.

5 Repeat step 3 at the other end, connecting the large-link chain instead of the S-hook. String a pearl on a head pin and use a wrapped loop to connect it to the free end of the chain.

materials

- PMC3 clay
- PMC3 syringe
- half-drilled 8–10mm pearl
- assorted 3–6mm pearls and Austrian crystals, and seed beads
- 6 in. (15cm) 22-gauge sterling silver round wire, half-hard
- 1 in. (2.5cm) 20- or 22-gauge fine silver round wire
- 4 in. (10cm) sterling silver large-link chain
- flexible beading wire
- 2 sterling silver cones
- sterling silver S-hook clasp
- 24-gauge sterling silver head pin
- **6** crimp beads
- **2** silk strands
- shell
- playing cards
- roller
- plastic mat
- Badger Balm
- small brush
- cup of water
- paper towel
- two-part epoxy
- flexible sanding pad
- round metal file
- X-acto knife or scalpel
- cocktail straw
- polishing pad
- roundnose pliers
- chainnose pliers
- crimping pliers
- side cutters
- liver of sulfur (optional)

tip

Opt for heavier gauge wire over lighter gauge for strength in your jewelry designs. If the heavier wire is too large for the pearl's hole, use a bead reamer to enlarge the hole.

Beaded Leaf Brooch

Leaves are a recurring motif in my designs, whether the piece focuses on traditional wirework or metal clay. In this piece, a leaf is imprinted directly onto metal clay, and then it is embellished with crystals and pearls. It also incorporates traditional wirework, with beads and wire woven through the leaf.

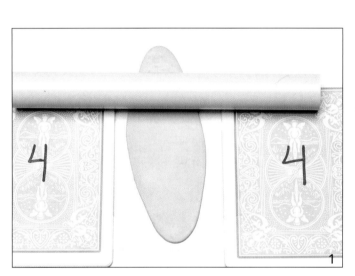

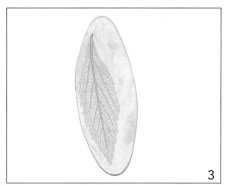

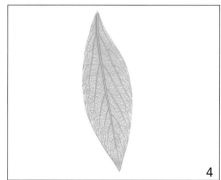

tip

If you live in a cold climate without access to fresh leaves during the winter, buy herbs from the grocery store. Try large mint or basil leaves.

Choose a leaf with a beautiful shape and well-defined veins. The spirea leaf I chose is long and elegantly shaped – well-suited for a brooch.

1 Roll the clay out to the thickness of four cards. Be sure to roll the clay out so that it will accommodate the leaf.

2-4 Place the leaf on the clay, vein side down **[2]**, and roll over to imprint it into the clay, making sure that your roller rests on the card stacks at all times. Carefully remove the leaf **[3]**, using tweezers if needed. Use an X-acto knife or scalpel to trim the excess clay around the leaf image **[4]**.

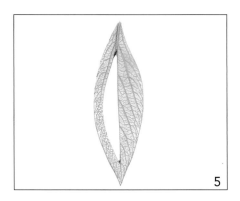

5

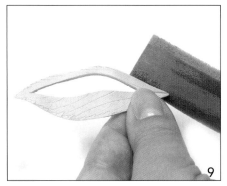

6

7

8

9

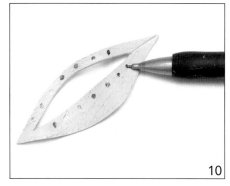

10

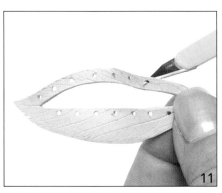

11

12

13

5-6 Using the X-acto knife, cut out an opening, leaving at least a 6mm margin of clay **[5]**. Shape the opening with a clean, slightly wet brush **[6]**.

7 Roll up two pieces of tissue paper and cover them with plastic wrap. Transfer the piece of clay from the plastic mat onto the plastic wrap. Gently reshape with the brush if necessary. Let the piece dry.

8-9 File the piece, using metal files to get into the corners of the opening. **[8]** Use the flexible sanding pad to finish the outside of the piece **[9]**.

10 With a pencil, mark the location of the holes. Make the

marks at least 5mm apart and at least 2mm from the edges. There should be an equal number of holes on each side of the opening.

11 Place the tip of the X-acto knife carefully on top of a pencil mark. Hold it at a right angle to the piece and gently rotate the knife without applying pressure. Then turn the piece over and repeat so that the hole is even on both sides. Continue until all of the holes have been carved out.

12-13 Embellish your piece with syringe. If the stem of the leaf has left a deep impression, you can fill it in with syringe as you're embellishing **[12, 13]**. Let the piece dry.

14-16 Attach the pin components to the back of the pin using syringe **[14]**, going around the base of each component at least twice. Be certain not to get any syringe inside of the component. Use a brush to remove any excess syringe around the components **[15]**. The space between the two components should be equal to the length of the pin **[16]**. Let the piece dry.

17-18 Fire your piece in vermiculite. The vermiculite supports the piece during firing, ensuring that the fired silver will retain its shape. Once fired, polish until the silver shines **[17]**. If you wish, use liver of sulfur to add a patina **[18]**.

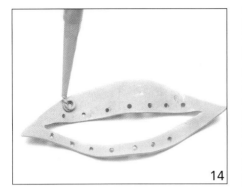

14

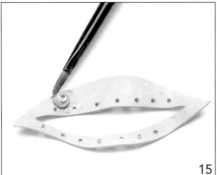

15

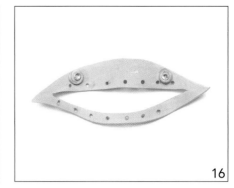

16

17

18

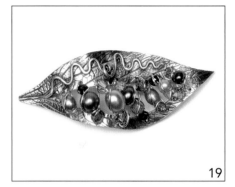

19

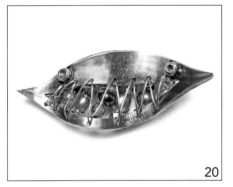

20

21

19 Starting on one side of the pin, begin lacing the wire through the holes. String an assortment of beads on the front pass, and then go back through a second time, winding the wire around the beads on the same wire. Continue to the next hole, threading the wire from the underside of the piece. Add beads on the next pass and continue with the same pattern. Finish by wrapping both ends of the wire around other pieces of wire on the back.

20-21 Screw in the pin components **[20]** and fasten the brooch **[21]**.

materials

- PMC3 clay
- PMC3 syringe
- assorted 6mm beads
- 24-gauge sterling silver round wire, dead soft
- pin component set
- large leaf with well-defined veins
- playing cards
- roller
- plastic mat
- Badger Balm
- small brush
- cup of water
- paper towel
- metal file or emery board
- flexible sanding pad
- X-acto knife or scalpel
- tissue paper
- plastic wrap
- pencil
- vermiculite
- polishing pad
- roundnose pliers
- chainnose pliers
- side cutters
- liver of sulfur (optional)

Starburst Pendant

All of the projects in this book are designed with beaders in mind, but this one is designed for a particular group: beaders who enjoy working with needle and thread. Embedding a brass screen in a metal clay piece creates an easy-to-use beading surface, perfect for adding bursts of colorful, sparkling crystals.

Often, syringe clay is used to set stones and add embellishments, but this piece is made entirely from syringe clay, giving it an airy, filigree-like framework.

Make the heart

1 Using pencil and paper, sketch a heart with a filigree-like pattern and a smaller heart in the center.

2 Cut a small heart, sized to match the smaller heart in your sketch, out of the brass screen with a cutter. Set aside.

3-4 Remove the pink tip of the syringe and wrap syringe two to three times around a well-greased straw to make a bail **[3]**. Use a brush to shape if needed **[4]**. Let the bail dry, remove it from the straw, and file away any sharp edges.

5 Tape a plastic sheet over the sketch, and grease the sheet. Place the brass screen heart on top of the sketch, over the smaller heart.

6-7 Create a frame around the brass screen heart using a tipless syringe **[6]**. Use a clean, slightly wet brush to gently push the syringe into and around the brass screen, concealing the cut edges **[7]**.

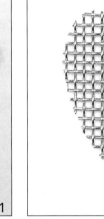

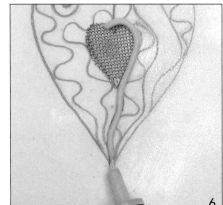

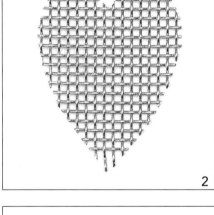

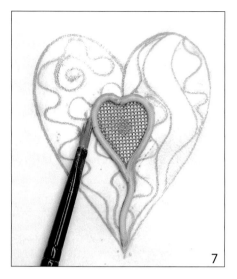

7

8

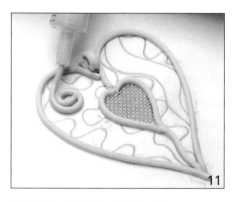

9

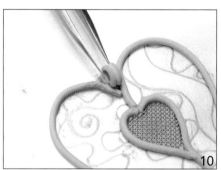

10

11

12

materials

- PMC3 syringe
- PMC3 paste (optional)
- size 13 silver Charlottes
- assorted 4mm Swarovski bicone crystals
- brass screen, 10 x 10mm
- Superlon or Nymo D beading thread
- small brush
- Badger Balm
- plastic mat
- cup of water
- paper towel
- pencil
- paper
- cocktail straw
- metal file
- flexible sanding pads
- beading needle, size 13
- scissors
- Scotch tape

8 Outline the larger heart with the tipless syringe, connecting it to the brass screen frame. With a clean, damp brush, smooth and shape the syringe outline.

9-10 Place a small blob of syringe into the cleft of the heart outline **[9]**. Moisten the dry bail and gently push it into the syringe **[10]**.

11-13 Fill in the design elements, using the tipless syringe **[11]**, making certain to interconnect the various elements with the frames **[12]**. Place the tip back on the syringe, and use the syringe with the tip to embellish and reinforce the piece **[13]**. Let the piece dry.

14-15 Once the piece has dried, remove it from the plastic sheet and sand and file it gently if needed **[14]**. If you wish, reinforce the back of the piece by painting it with paste **[15]**. Let the paste dry.

16 Fire according to the manufacturer's instructions. Polish until the silver shines.

Embellish the heart with beads

1 Thread a needle with 1–2 yd. (.9–1.8m) of Nymo D or Superlon. Leaving a 6-in. (15cm) tail, tie the thread to the outer edge of the screen with a square knot.

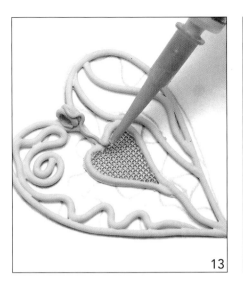 13

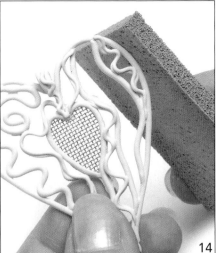 14

 15

tip

It is helpful to have a dedicated syringe without a tip instead of taking the tip off and putting it back on. This will help prevent the clay from drying inside the tip.

 16

2 With the thread exiting the front of the pendant, pick up five Charlottes, a 4mm crystal, and a Charlotte. Skip the last bead, and sew back through the crystal, the five Charlottes, and the screen. Sew up through the next square of the screen along the edge. Repeat around the edge, adding thread as needed.

3 After completing the first row, come up through the screen approximately ⅛ in. (3mm) from the edge. Continue adding beads as in step 2, but decrease the number of Charlottes to three or four instead of five. Fill in the center as desired, decreasing the number of Charlottes to one or two, until the center is full.

4 Secure the thread to the screen with a square knot, sew up through a branch of fringe, and trim. Thread your needle on the 6-in. tail from step 1, sew up through a branch of fringe, and trim.

Silver-spiraled Glass Beads

More ideas p. 96

The spiral is an ancient symbol of the cycles of growth, change, and life's journey. These art glass beads are the perfect background for syringe spirals.

Sterling silver chain makes the beads the focus of the necklace and gives the earrings a wonderful sense of movement.

Embellish the beads

1 With clay paste and a small brush, paint the inside of each hole in the five beads. Let the first layer dry and apply another layer.

2-4 Use the syringe to create a spiral radiating from the center of each bead and ending on the outer edge of the bead **[2]**. Make certain to connect the syringe to the painted center of the bead by tapping with a clean, slightly wet brush **[3]**. Let the piece dry. Turn it over and repeat steps 2 and 3 on the other side, making certain that the two spirals meet at the outer edge of the bead **[4]**. Let the piece dry.

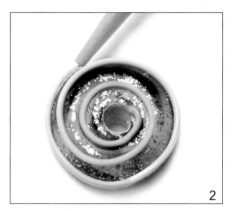

5

6

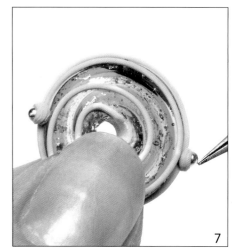

7

8

9

10

materials

- PMC3 syringe
- PMC3 paste
- **5** 15–20mm lampwork rondelles with large holes (by Dee Howl)
- casting grain
- sterling silver small-link chain
- 4–5mm sterling silver beads
- 22-gauge sterling silver wire, half-hard
- sterling silver ear wires
- sterling silver toggle clasp
- cup of water
- small brush
- paper towel
- side cutters
- tweezers
- polishing pad
- roundnose pliers
- chainnose pliers
- side cutters
- liver of sulfur (optional)

5-9 Position the casting grain around the circumference of each bead. Think of each bead as the face of a clock. Set the first casting grain at twelve o'clock by moistening the portion of the spiral you're working on with a slightly wet brush. Make a blob that straddles the spiral. With tweezers, set the casting grain on top of the blob and carefully push it in as far as it will go **[5, 6]**. Set the second casting grain at six o'clock **[7]**, the third at three o'clock **[8]**, and the fourth at nine o'clock. Now you can fill in between the first four pieces of casting grain by adding more casting grain at similar intervals **[9]**. (You'll likely end up with more than 12 pieces of casting grain around the bead; I show 15.)

10 Fire the pieces at a temperature no higher than 1300°F (704°C). Let the kiln cool gradually. Do not open the kiln door or crash

cool the pieces. Once fired, polish the beads until the silver shines. If you wish, use liver of sulfur to add a patina.

Make the necklace

1 Cut six pieces of silver chain long enough to go through a spiral bead and wrap around the sides.

2 Cut a 3-in. (7.6cm) piece of 22-gauge wire, and make the first half of a wrapped loop at one end. String a 4–5mm silver bead and make the first half of a wrapped loop after the bead, leaving enough space on each side of the bead to finish the wraps later. Repeat for a total of ten wrapped loop units.

3 Wrap a chain piece around a spiral bead and slide both end links onto a loop of a wrapped-loop

unit. Finish the wraps. Repeat with another spiral bead, this time sliding the end chain links into the remaining loop of the wrapped loop unit. Finish the wraps.

4 Wrap a chain around the other side of the last spiral bead added, and string the end links onto a wrapped loop unit. Finish the wraps.

5 Attach a wrapped loop unit to the remaining loop and finish the wraps. Repeat to attach a third wrapped loop unit after the spiral bead.

6 Repeat steps 3–5 on the other side of the center spiral bead.

7 Add the length of the clasp, the two remaining wrapped loop units, and the linked components. Subtract this total from the desired length and divide by two. Cut two pieces of chain to this length.

8 Attach an end link of chain to a remaining loop on the linked components, and finish the wraps.

9 Attach a remaining wrapped loop unit to the end of the chain and finish the wraps. Attach one half of a clasp to the other loop and finish the wraps.

10 Repeat steps 8 and 9 at the other end of the necklace.

Make the earrings

1 Cut a length of chain long enough to go through a spiral bead and wrap around the sides.

2 Cut a 3-in. (7.6cm) piece of 22-gauge wire and make the first half of a wrapped loop on one end.

3 String a spiral bead onto a chain, string both end links onto the loop, and finish the wraps. String a silver bead on the wire, and make a wrapped loop.

4 Open the loop of an ear wire, string the earring, and close the loop. Make a second earring to match the first.

tip

Purchased casting grain comes in random shapes and sizes. When you have a project that requires uniform casting grain, it's often easiest to make it yourself by cutting equally sized pieces of fine silver wire and heating them with a torch until they become round.

Calla Lily Suite

The simple, graceful lines of the calla lily are inspiring to artists and jewelers. I chose to sculpt each component by hand in order to give the pieces a strong three-dimensional aspect.

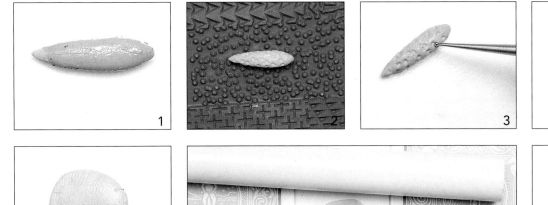

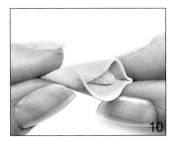

Make the pendant

1 To make a stamen, roll a short coil of clay approximately 12–14mm long and 3–4mm in diameter. Shape it so that one of the ends is more tapered than the other.

2-3 Texture the stamen by rolling it on a stamp [2] or use a small ball stylus [3]. Let the piece dry.

4-6 Roll a small ball of clay, using approximately 2–3 grams [4]. Slightly flatten the ball of clay with your fingers [5]. Then roll it to the thickness of three cards (change direction while rolling in order to roll out a round piece) [6].

7 Brush the center of the rolled piece of clay with paste and place the stamen in the middle.

8 Fold one side of the rolled piece to partially cover the stamen, adding more paste if necessary. Attach the side by gently pushing it with a brush.

9-11 Fold the other side of the rolled out piece to partially cover both the first side and the stamen, again adding more paste if necessary. Attach the side by gently pushing on it with your brush [9]. Pinch the top of the calla lily with your fingers to close the gap, and pinch the bottom of the calla lily with your fingers to give it a flower shape [10]. You can also shape and slightly open the calla lily with your brush [11].

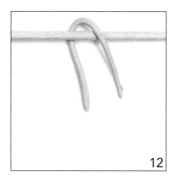

12

13

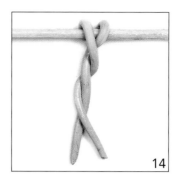

14

15

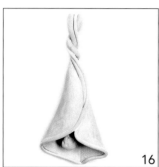

16

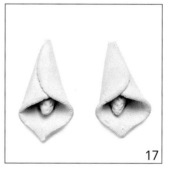

17

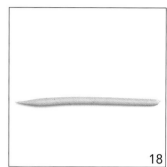

18

materials

- PMC3 clay
- PMC3 paste
- 4–6mm pearls
- 18 in. (45.7cm) 22-gauge sterling silver round wire, half-hard
- sterling silver ear wires
- sterling silver jump rings
- sterling silver toggle clasp
- small brush
- cup of water
- paper towel
- plastic mat
- roller
- coil roller
- playing cards
- Badger Balm
- cocktail straw
- ball stylus or unmounted rubber stamp mat
- X-acto knife or scalpel
- metal file or emery board
- flexible sanding pad
- roundnose pliers
- chainnose pliers
- side cutters
- polishing pad
- liver of sulfur (optional)

Add a simple bail to the pendant

Roll out a thin coil approximately 30mm long. Drape the coil over a greased straw or skewer **[12]** and attach the coil to the front and the back of the calla lily with paste or syringe **[13]**.

Option: Add a twisted bail to the pendant

Roll out a thin coil approximately 60mm long. Wrap the coil around a greased straw or skewer twice so that the ends of the coil are approximately the same length. Twist the ends of the coil two or three times **[14]** and attach them to the front and the back of the calla lily with paste or syringe **[15]**. Embellish with syringe **[16]**.

Make the earring components

1 Follow steps 1–11 above to create two calla lilies that are mirror images of each other. Dry the pieces **[17]**.

2 Roll out a thin, 15–20mm coil for each earring **[18]**.

3 Make a loop by bringing the two ends of the coil together **[19]**. Repeat with the second coil.

4 Moisten the dried calla lily components **[20]** and set them on top of the coil loops, slightly pushing them into the loops. Dry the pieces **[21]**.

5 File and sand the pieces **[22]**, and embellish them with syringe **[23]**. Dry the pieces **[24]**.

Make the bracelet components

1 Create five calla lily components. Dry the pieces.

2 Repeat steps 2–4 of "Make the earring components." Let the pieces dry.

3 To make the hole at the bottom of each component, place the tip of the X-acto knife approximately 2–3mm from the bottom edge of the calla lily. Hold it at a right angle to the piece and gently rotate the knife without applying pressure **[25]**. Then turn the piece over and repeat so that the hole is even on both sides. Continue until all of the holes have been carved **[26]**.

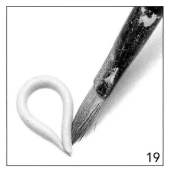

19

20

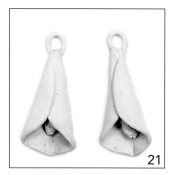

21

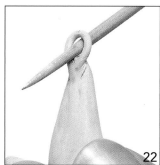

22

23

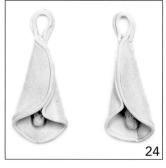

24

25

26

tip

When designing a sculptural piece, I find it's helpful to practice with polymer clay. Its consistency is similar to metal clay, and I don't have to worry about the clay drying out.

Fire and polish the components

Let all of the components dry completely, then fire according to the manufacturer's instructions. Polish the fired pieces until the silver shines. If you wish, use liver of sulfur to add a patina.

Complete the bracelet

1 Cut four 3-in. (7.6cm) pieces of 22-gauge wire, and make the first half of a wrapped loop at one end of each.

2 Attach the loop of a wire to the stem of a calla lily component, and finish the wraps. String a pearl on the wire, and make the first half of a wrapped loop. Attach the loop to the tip of another calla lily component.

3 Repeat step 2 three times.

4 Test for fit. If the bracelet is within ½ in. (1.3cm) of the desired length, attach one half of a clasp to each end component with a jump ring. If more length is needed, make two more wrapped loop units. Attach one loop of a unit to a calla lily component and the other loop to one half of a clasp, and finish the wraps. Repeat on the other end.

Complete the earrings

1 Cut a 3-in. (7.6cm) piece of 22-gauge wire and make the first half of a wrapped loop. String a pearl on the wire, and make the first half of a wrapped loop. Attach the second loop to a calla lily component and finish the wraps.

2 Slide the loop of an ear wire onto the first loop and finish the wraps. Make a second earring to match the first.

Hollow Donut Bead

More ideas p. 98

Cork clay and metal clay paste often are used together to create hollow beads and vessels. Donuts make beautiful, versatile necklace centerpieces. The offset holes in this piece allow it to hang gracefully, whether from a chain or a beaded necklace. And, because it's hollow, it looks solid and substantial, yet it's lightweight and very wearable.

Make the donut bead

1-2 Flatten a large piece of cork clay **[1]**, and place it into the large round clay cutter. Roll over the cork clay with the roller **[2]**, leaving one side flat and one side rounded.

3 Use the small round clay cutter to punch a hole in the center of the larger piece.

4 Insert toothpicks into the donut-shaped cork clay as shown. Let the cork clay dry completely.

5-6 Once the cork is dry, begin applying paste **[5]**. Apply 10 to 14 coats of paste, making certain to let each coat dry thoroughly before you paint the next coat. Let the piece dry **[6]**.

1

2

3

4

5

6

7

8

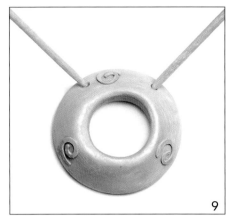

9

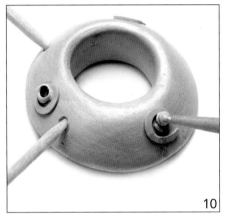

10

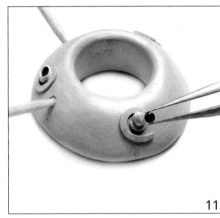

11

12

7 File carefully around the holes to remove excess dried paste. Sand the piece thoroughly to create a smooth texture.

8-9 Laminate a piece of sheet clay by folding it in half and gluing it together using Elmer's glue. Let the glue dry, and use a paper punch to punch spirals out of the sheet **[8]**. Use Elmer's glue to attach the spirals to the donut bead **[9]**.

tip

If the cork clay begins to dry out as you're working with it, simply moisten your fingertips with a bit of water and smooth it out.

10-11 Create a syringe blob in the center of each spiral **[10]** and set a CZ in it **[11]**.

12-14 Use a pencil with light pressure to mark the donut where you want to add syringe clay embellishment **[12]**. Use syringe to trace over the pencil lines **[13]**. Make certain to embellish around the holes. Let the piece dry **[14]**.

15-16 Fire the piece according to the manufacturer's instructions. The cork burns away during firing, leaving just the hollow silver shape. Polish the fired piece until the silver shines **[15]**. If you wish, use liver of sulfur to apply a patina **[16]**.

Make the necklace

1 Center the donut on five 20-in. (51cm) pieces of flexible beading wire.

2 String an assortment of beads onto each strand **[17]** as desired, making all the strands the same length.

3 Cut a 3-in. (7.6cm) piece of 22-gauge wire and make a wrapped loop. String a crimp bead on one end of each strand of beading wire. Take all five strands through the wrapped loop, and then go back through the crimp beads and a few more beads on each strand. Crimp the crimp beads and trim the excess beading wire. String a cone on the 22-gauge wire, and make the first half of a wrapped loop above the cone. Attach the loop to the hook clasp and finish the wraps. Repeat on the other side of the necklace, attaching the wrapped loop to an end of the large-link chain.

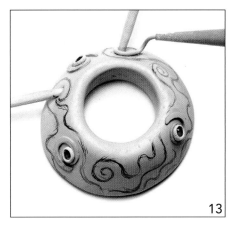

13

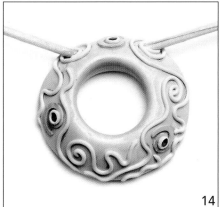

14

15

16

17

4 String a crystal on a head pin and make the first half of a wrapped loop. Attach the loop to the end of the large-link chain and finish the wraps.

tip

When polishing your piece in a magnetic polisher, it is helpful to insert pieces of toothpick in the holes to prevent the polishing media from becoming lodged in the openings.

materials

- PMC3 paste
- PMC3 syringe
- PMC+ sheet
- cork clay
- **3** 2mm kiln-ready CZs
- 6 in. (15cm) 22-gauge sterling silver round wire, half-hard
- flexible beading wire
- assorted Thai silver cylindrical beads and 2mm semi-precious stone rondelles
- **2** sterling silver cones
- sterling silver hook clasp
- 4 in. (10.2cm) sterling silver large-link chain
- **10** crimp beads
- 2-in. (5cm) 24-gauge sterling silver head pin
- small brush
- tweezers
- cup of water
- paper towel
- paper punch
- small round clay cutter (approximately 20mm)
- large round clay cutter (approximately 35mm)
- roller
- metal file or emery board
- toothpicks
- Elmer's glue
- flexible sanding pads
- polishing pad
- roundnose pliers
- chainnose pliers
- side cutters
- crimping pliers
- liver of sulfur (optional)

Sea Treasure Necklace

More ideas p. 99

Transform a seashell into a beautiful pendant by creating a mold to capture all of the shell's unique textures. This clean and elegant design makes a stunning, lightweight bead with great design potential.

I chose a seashell to make my mold, but you also can use vintage glass or brass stamps, buttons, glass cabochons, or anything else that's deep and highly textured.

Make the pendant

Choose an object from which to make a mold.

1-2 Measure out equal parts of the two-part mold putty [1] and combine them. Knead them together long enough to make the color uniform [2]. Take the prepared mold material and slightly flatten it, making certain that it remains thick enough to accommodate the thickness of the shell.

3 Press the shell evenly into the mold material. Leave the shell in the material until the mold sets. Once the mold has set, lift the shell out of the mold. Now the mold is ready to be used.

4 Roll the clay out to the thickness of five cards. The size of the rolled-out clay should be larger than the mold (the deeper the mold, the larger the size of the rolled clay).

1

2

3

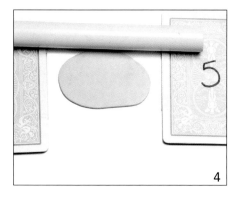

4

5

6

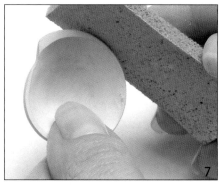

7

8

9

10

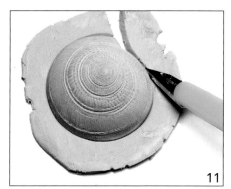

11

12

5-7 Press the rolled piece of clay firmly into the mold **[5]**. Carefully trim the excess clay **[6]**. Let the piece dry, and remove it from the mold once drying is complete. If needed, file and sand the dried piece **[7]**.

8-12 Roll out a piece of clay to the thickness of four cards and slightly larger than the

> ## tip
>
> When working with two-part mold material, I find it convenient to use measuring spoons or cups to precisely measure the amounts for consistent results.

base of the shell **[8]**. Paint the piece with paste **[9]**. Moisten the edge of the dry top piece and press it into the rolled piece until it sinks in about halfway **[10]**. Trim the excess clay around the shape **[11]**. Let the piece dry. If needed, file and sand the edges when dried **[12]**.

13-14 Using an X-acto knife, carve out two holes in the back of the piece **[13]**. File and shape them with the round file **[14]**.

15-17 Carve a hole for the CZ with the X-acto knife by holding it perpendicular to the piece **[15]**. Squeeze a blob of syringe over the hole **[16]**, and use tweezers to set the CZ **[17]**. Let the piece dry.

18-19 Fire the piece according to the manufacturer's instructions, and polish the fired piece until the silver shines **[18]**. If you wish, use liver of sulfur to apply a patina **[19]**.

Make the necklace

1 Center the pendant on three 20-in. (51cm) strands of flexible beading wire.

2 String beads as desired on each strand until the necklace is within 1 in. (2.5cm) of the desired length.

3 Cut a 3-in. (7.6cm) piece of 22-gauge wire and make a wrapped loop at one end. String a crimp

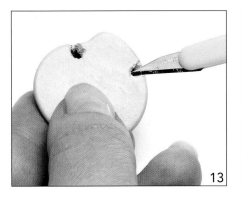

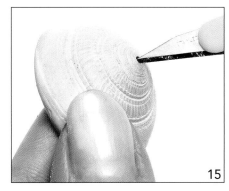

13 14 15

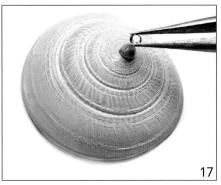

16 17

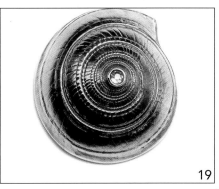

18 19

materials

- PMC3 clay
- PMC3 syringe
- PMC3 paste
- item to make a mold from
- 4mm kiln-ready CZ
- 6 in. (15cm) 22-gauge sterling silver round wire
- **3** 2-in. (5cm) 24-gauge sterling silver head pins
- flexible beading wire
- sterling silver cones
- sterling silver large-link chain
- sterling silver hook clasp
- assortment of 2–6mm pearls and silver beads
- **6** crimp beads
- two-part mold putty
- roller
- plastic mat
- playing cards
- Badger Balm
- small brush
- cup of water
- paper towel
- tweezers
- round metal file
- flexible sanding pads
- X-acto knife or scalpel
- polishing pad
- roundnose pliers
- chainnose pliers
- side cutters
- crimping pliers
- liver of sulfur (optional)

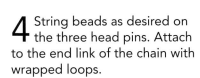

bead on one end of each strand of beading wire, and take all three wires through the wrapped loop. Go back through the crimp beads and a few more beads on each strand, and crimp the crimp beads. String a cone and a bead on the 22-gauge wire, and make the first half of a wrapped loop above the bead. Attach it to the hook, and finish the wraps. Repeat on the other side, attaching the wrapped loop to an end link of chain.

4 String beads as desired on the three head pins. Attach to the end link of the chain with wrapped loops.

Add variety and extra sparkle to a ring by choosing varied shapes, sizes, and colors of CZs.

More *Garden Ring* ideas

Adapt the ring techniques to make garden pendants. If you curve the clay for dimension, support it with tissue paper as it dries.

With a combination of techniques, you can design a wide variety of earrings. Add leaves and CZs to imprinted clay, set larger CZs and hold them in place with syringe, or connect multiple leaves with curves of syringe.

Create fantastic filigree "hair" around a face cab with syringe. Leave openings in the syringe where wire and bead embellishments can be added after firing.

The porcelain components used for these earrings have holes at the top. Use the riveting technique (see Riveted Bead project, p. 28) front to back on the components and embed a fine silver wire for the hanging loop.

More *Porcelain Cabochon* ideas

Use stamps and leaves to create interesting backgrounds for the cabochons.

Porcelain face cabochons by Melanie Brooks; geometric components by Marsha Neal

Stamping and twisting the clay can result in a variety of intriguing shapes.

More *Twisted* ideas

This technique lends itself well to making a cuff bracelet.

Using different types of shells as molds, you can create many different components.

Another exciting design variable is the color and shape of the pearls you choose.

Explore the variety of nature's leaf shapes. Create different looks with the type of beads and embellishments you add.

More *Beaded Leaf* ideas

Massed leaves make a striking necklace. For the earrings, small curled leaves and pearls sway on wrapped loops.

In this variation, I pierced a circular pattern of holes and attached small gemstone donuts with wire.

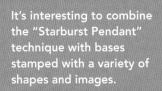

It's interesting to combine the "Starburst Pendant" technique with bases stamped with a variety of shapes and images.

We started with a heart; now try other shapes like petals, ovals, and others.

Enclose CZ drops in a spiral of syringe, then add bails to create necklace and earring components.

Put two dichroic cabochons back to back and enclose them in a spiral to create a caged bead.

More *Silver Spiral* ideas

I made this ring using both the spiraling and the riveting techniques.

Lampwork bead by Jeff Plath

Always make cuff brace-
lets 10–12% larger than
the finished size to allow
for shrinkage.

Try using a CZ drop as a stamen.

A long clay coil becomes a free-
form pin.

Cut clay into heart shapes to make this anthurium set.

Large pieces of casting grain embellish this hollow piece.

Cork clay makes it easy to create hollow focal beads in a variety of shapes.

More *Hollow Form* ideas

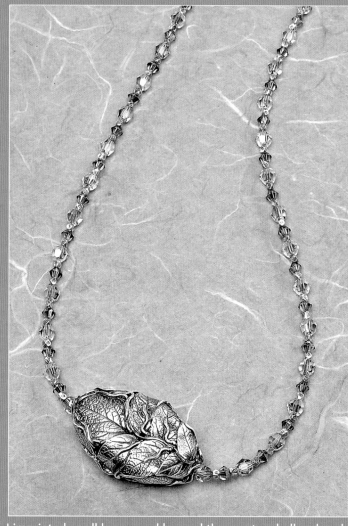

I imprinted small leaves and layered them onto a hollow bead, then added syringe embellishment.

To make this piece, roll out the clay and push the center of it into the mold. Trim the sides, leaving as much or as little clay as you want to frame the image.

A vintage cabochon was the mold for this set.

Make your own molds from the ocean's treasures, like shells and sea stars.

Materials and Tools

If metal clay is a material that is new to you, this section is a good place to become familiar with the supplies you'll need to begin working with this versatile medium. Those who are more familiar will find it a handy reference, with tips and techniques, some helpful wireworking tips, and a firing chart.

Although metal clay can be expensive, the tools needed for shaping, sanding, and finishing it are not. This is a big advantage that sets metal clay apart from traditional work in precious metal: Because the clay is soft and pliable, you do not need drills, saws, and other power equipment to make it take shape.

Materials

Metal clay basics

What exactly is metal clay?

Metal clay is relatively new to the jewelry-making community but has gained an ever-growing following in its first decade. This revolutionary material consists of small particles of precious metals – currently either silver or gold, though testing is underway for other metals – that are suspended in an organic binder. The binder gives metal clay its malleable elasticity; when fired, the organic element burns away, leaving 99.9% pure precious metal in its hardened form.

Two product lines are available to the artist – Precious Metal Clay (PMC) and Art Clay. As a PMC Senior Instructor, I use PMC in my work, but both product lines are readily available, have similar properties, and come with complete firing directions.

Metal clay is available in four main forms: lump clay, syringe clay, paste, and sheet clay. See Resources, p. 111, for metal clay products sources.

Lump clay

The most common form of metal clay, lump clay can be rolled into thin sheets, textured, imprinted, rolled into ropes, sculpted, or shaped by hand. Kiln-safe cubic zirconias (CZs) and lab-created gemstones can be set into it and safely fired.

Lump clay has a low proportion of water in it and can dry out quickly, which makes it difficult to mold or manipulate if it has begun to harden. Keep unused portions covered with plastic wrap and moisten the portion you're working with by periodically spraying it with a mister.

Syringe clay

Syringe clay comes in a syringe applicator (hence its name). It is watered-down clay that is squeezed out and applied, much like using a cake-decorating tool. It is used to set stones and casting grain, and to create bails, lines, dots, spirals, and any other shape you can envision. Its possibilities are limitless, particularly if you have a steady hand. Syringes come filled and ready to use.

Paste

Paste is clay mixed with water to the consistency of thick paint. It is used to paint on organic items such as leaves and pods to re-create them in metal. Paste is also used in conjunction with cork clay to create hollow beads and vessels. Paste can be purchased commercially or made by recycling leftover pieces of unfired metal clay.

To make paste, put your leftover pieces of clay into an airtight glass or plastic container (not metal) and add a little water. In just a few hours you will have paste. If you add too much water and your paste is too thin, simply leave the container open and let the extra water evaporate. Some metal clay products are not compatible, so it's best to label the type of paste in a specific container.

Make the consistency of your paste fit your project. You can thin it by adding water; the resulting paste is commonly called slip and is often used as a glue to adhere pieces of unfired metal clay together.

Sheet clay

Unlike the other metal clay products, which are water-based, sheet clay is oil-based. When you open its packaging, it doesn't dry out – which means you have unlimited working time. This product can be treated much like paper, and those readers who are scrapbookers will likely have a variety of paper punches that can be used with sheet clay. Originally intended for origami, it can be folded perfectly or cut with scissors to form intricate shapes.

Sheet clay does not stick to itself, so in order to construct pieces out of it, use Elmer's glue or syringe clay in small quantities. Avoid water, which can melt and distort sheet clay. If you must use paste, make it very thick to minimize the amount of water that can be absorbed.

Precious Metal Clay product line

The projects presented in this book are based on the PMC family. The Art Clay line offers similar products. The following is an explanation of specific PMC products and their uses.

PMC Standard products

PMC Standard metal clay is available in lump form only, which means its uses are limited because of the lack of compatible products within the PMC Standard line. Essentially, if you want to work with PMC Standard, you'll need to make your own PMC Standard paste and forego adding syringe or sheet clay to your piece.

When fired, PMC Standard shrinks approximately 30% in volume – more than any other PMC (or Art Clay) product due to its large amount of organic binder.

The high shrinkage rate of PMC Standard presents both advantages and disadvantages. PMC Standard is well suited for projects involving carving. Its high quantity of binder makes this metal clay very easy to carve when dry, unlike other metal clay products, which can be so brittle when dry that they crack or break during carving. This product is also an excellent choice when you are working with a busy design;

when fired, the design will shrink to suitably intricate detail.

The high rate of shrinkage can be a disadvantage when exact sizing is important, such as in ring projects.

PMC+ sheet clay

PMC+ sheet clay is thin and can be folded like paper without cracking. Its shrinkage rate is 10–12%. This form contains no water, so it remains workable much longer than other forms of PMC.

PMC3 products

PMC3 is the best product to use for making rings because it is less porous than other metal clay products; this means it's harder after firing and can withstand the heavy wear rings receive. The PMC3 product line has a shrinkage rate of approximately 12% in volume, the same as PMC+ sheet, and you can combine PMC3 with PMC+ if you fire the finished piece at the PMC+ temperature (which excludes the use of glass).

The primary difference between the two lines is that PMC3 products were developed as a low-fire metal clay, allowing the use of dichroic glass in metal clay projects. PMC3 products are available in lump, syringe and paste forms.

PMC3 paste works well as paste or slip. In addition, it is the best product for making repairs or adding elements to already-fired pieces.

PMC Gold products

PMC Gold, a lump clay form, can be formed, imprinted, cut into shapes, and so on – just like the silver clays. This strong and durable gold clay is a 22-karat alloy of gold and silver with a shrinkage rate of approximately 12%. It can be used by itself, or with any of the PMC silver products (PMC+ and PMC3 are preferred because they most closely match the firing schedule and shrinkage rate). Like the silver clays, PMC Gold also can be used to make paste by adding water.

Aura 22 is a liquid 22-karat gold paste that can be used to paint on fired and unfired metal clay pieces. For a light gold, use one layer. For a darker gold, use two to three layers. Let it dry thoroughly between coats.

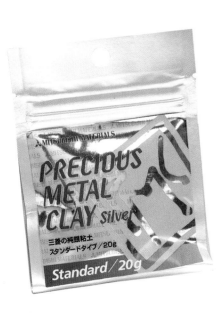

Tools

Although metal clay is relatively expensive, the tools you need to work with it are not. You may find some of the basic items around the house, perhaps in your kitchen, craft room, or garage. It's a good idea to round up all the tools you'll need for metal clay and keep them together, reserving any kitchen items exclusively for metal clay use.

Shaping tools

Any surface that touches metal clay must be lightly greased so that the metal clay won't stick to it. This includes the plastic mat and roller you use to start a project as well as any miscellaneous tools you use (such as straws for making bails). A natural hand emollient such as **Badger Balm** works well, as does **olive oil**.

A **ball stylus** is a shaping tool that can be used to create textures or to push down on clay in place of your finger to avoid leaving a fingerprint.

The **blending tool**, sometimes called a wipeout tool, blends seams in metal clay; it's also used to clean up debris on glass.

A **coil roller** is a piece of Plexiglas or acrylic used to roll clay into smooth, uniform coils.

Use a **craft knife**, such as an X-acto, or **scalpel** to cut clay and to make small holes.

The **needle stylus** is used to make small holes or to mark spots for later hole placement. It also works well to sign the back of your pieces. In a pinch, use a very sharp pencil in place of a stylus.

Use a small artists' **paintbrush** to apply water to clay. Dampen it to shape clay and syringe, to smooth surfaces, and to apply slip. Use it dry on newly sanded pieces to brush off debris.

A must to wipe your brushes on, **paper towels** are also used to wick away excess water if you accidentally put too much on your piece. Simply touch a corner of the towel to the wet portion and watch the water soak upward; avoid wiping your wet piece as you could mar the surface decoration.

Create **plastic work mats** by cutting apart clear report covers from stores that sell office or school supplies. Always remember to lightly grease your plastic mat before working on it. If the plastic mat becomes scored in the process of cutting out metal clay shapes, dispose of it and use a new mat – otherwise, scratches on the mat will transfer to the back of your piece.

Use **playing cards** to control the thickness of a piece of clay as it is rolled out. A standard thickness is three cards; you can tape sets of three cards together to make counting easier in projects that require many cards. Some projects may require single cards.

Used to smoothly roll out metal clay to a specific thickness (usually measured in a number of playing cards), a **roller** may be as simple as a piece of PVC pipe (available at hardware stores) or an acrylic brayer (available at art-supply stores). Always grease it lightly before use.

Select a **ruler** that has both millimeters and inches. Beads are generally measured in millimeters.

Straws (drinking and cocktail), scalpel, craft knife, fine-tip paintbrush, roller

Badger Balm, small plastic work mat, playing cards, acrylic coil roller

Ruler (inches/millimeters), blending tool, needle stylus, ball stylus, tweezers

Use small **straws** or coffee stirrers to create dainty bails and **drinking straws** for larger bails. Straws also can be used to punch holes in clay. Be sure to use the same straw when making components of the same size.

Use **tweezers** to pick up and set CZs and casting grain, and to remove leaves and stems after imprinting them into clay. You also can use them to remove polished pieces from the magnetic polisher.

Keep a cup of **water** next to you while working with metal clay. Use it to wash and wet your brush, keep your syringe fresh, and add to your paste if needed.

Abrasive tools

Emery boards are used to file flat edges and surfaces.

Use **flexible sanding pads** to file dimensional pieces such as vessels, beads, and rings.

Use **metal files** to file irregularly shaped pieces, or to get into small crevices that cannot be reached with an emery board or flexible sanding pad. For projects like those in this book, I keep two sets handy: a set of small and a set of extra-small files.

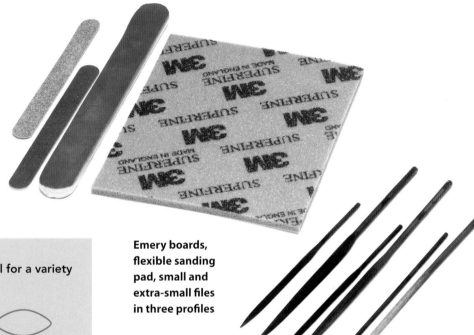

Emery boards, flexible sanding pad, small and extra-small files in three profiles

Metal file profiles
I find these profiles are the most useful for a variety of metal clay projects.

 full round
 half round
 double half round

Finishing tools and products

Burnishers give a bright polish to the high spots on your fired piece.

Liver of sulfur, an unpleasant-smelling but nontoxic substance, gives a patina or an antique finish to fired pieces. It is available ready-to-use in liquid form, or you can buy lump form and mix small pieces with warm water.

Polishing pads remove most of the liver of sulfur, leaving color only in the low spots of the piece.

If you do not have access to a tumbler or magnetic polisher, use a **steel brush** to polish your piece to a high shine after firing.

Polishing cloths give a final shine to any fired piece, whether a patina has been applied or not. No polishing compound is necessary.

Steel brush, burnisher, liver of sulfur, polishing cloth and pad

Project-specific tools

While many metal clay projects can be made with just the shaping and finishing tools mentioned earlier, some require more-specific tools.

To add texture to clay, use **acrylic texture sheets, brass plates, lace,** and **unmounted rubber stamp mats**.

Clay cutters and **paper punches** are used to punch shapes out of clay.

Cork clay is a moldable substance used to create hollow-form pieces such as vessels and beads. When the piece is fired, the cork clay burns away, leaving the same shape in hollow silver.

Ring forms called **HattieS Patties** are used to retain the shape and size of a ring while it is being fired; they are not reusable.

Use a sharp No. 2 **pencil** to draw designs on dry PMC Standard prior to carving it. You can also draw lightly on PMC Sheet with a pencil.

A **step ring mandrel** is used to form rings to the proper size and to hold the ring as you're working on it. You can make a **rest** to support the ring mandrel (or other tools, like a straw) out of two-part molding compound. Form a ball and then press the mandrel or a dowel into it.

When making rings, wrap a small piece of paper or a Post-it note around the mandrel, then cover it with **invisible tape**. Grease the tape before forming the ring around it. The paper and the tape will slide off the mandrel easily for sanding and firing.

A **tissue blade** makes long, straight cuts without distorting clay shapes.

Strong **two-part epoxy** is recommended for use with jewelry. To hold PMC+ sheet in place, use a small amount of **Elmer's glue**.

Two-part molding compound is used to create molds. Mix equal amounts of the two parts until a uniform color is reached, then press an object into the molding compound.

U- and V-shaped carving tools are primarily used with PMC Standard, because the high amount of binder in this product makes it well suited to carving. Hold the carving tools at a slight angle and apply gentle pressure as you follow your designs. To make the design deeper, go over the carving again, removing more material. The carving tools are sharp, so exercise caution.

Wood skewers are helpful in creating hollow beads and vessels. They also can be used to punch holes. **Toothpicks** come in handy too, for punching holes or for forming very small bails.

Wood skewers and toothpicks; texturing tools (lace, brass plates, acrylic texture sheets, rubber stamp mats); punch and clay cutters; two-part silicone molding compound; cork clay; adhesives

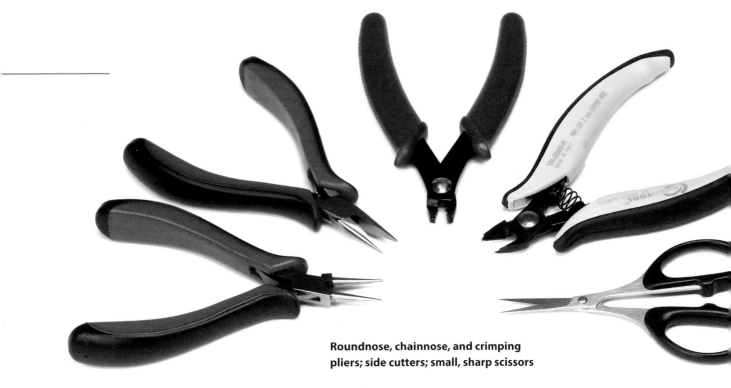

Roundnose, chainnose, and crimping pliers; side cutters; small, sharp scissors

Pliers and scissors

Roundnose pliers are essential for shaping wire and creating loops, including wrapped loops, a common connection for adding components such as clasps. The round jaws ensure your wirework has smooth curves.

The angled jaws of **chainnose pliers** are useful for bending wire into right angles and opening the loops on ear wires. They also are used with roundnose pliers to make wrapped loops (see sidebar on p. 108 to learn this technique).

Crimping pliers have grooved jaws and are used to tighten crimp beads or tubes around flexible beading wire for a professional finish to necklace and bracelet ends (see sidebar below).

Side cutters are very effective for cutting wire.

Sheet clay can be cut with **scissors**, provided they are small and sharp. You also can use decorative-edge scissors to create fancy edges.

Carving tool; ring mandrel and HattieS Pattie; tissue blade

Crimping
To crimp a necklace or bracelet end, position the crimp bead in the notch closest to the crimping pliers' handle [a]. Separate the wires and firmly squeeze the crimp [b]. Move the crimp into the notch at the pliers' tip and hold the crimp as shown. Squeeze the crimp bead, folding it in half at the indentation [c]. Tug the clasp to make sure the folded crimp is secure [d].

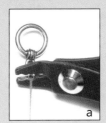

a

b

c

d

Making a wrapped loop

To make a wrapped loop, trim the wire 1¼ in. (3.2cm) above the bead. With the tip of your chainnose pliers, grasp the wire directly above the bead and make a right-angle bend [**a**]. Position the jaws of the roundnose pliers in the bend [**b**]. Bring the wire over the top jaw of the roundnose pliers [**c**]. Reposition the pliers so the lower jaw fits snugly in the loop and wrap the wire down and around the bottom of the pliers [**d**]. This is the first half of the wrapped loop. Grasp the loop with chainnose pliers [**e**]. Wrap the wire tail around the stem, covering the stem between the loop and the top bead. Trim the excess wrapping wire and press the end close to the wraps with chainnose or crimping pliers [**f**].

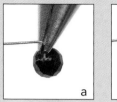 a
 b
 c
 d
 e
 f

Setting a stone

When setting a CZ in syringe or lump clay, set the widest part of the stone, the girdle, just below the level of the clay for the most secure setting.

girdle

METAL CLAY FIRING CHART

Fire longer at a higher temperature for the most shrinkage and durability

TYPE OF CLAY	MINIMUM FIRING TEMPERATURE	MINIMUM FIRING TIME	SHRINKAGE	FIRING METHOD
PMC3	1290°F/700°C 1200°F/650°C 1110°F/600°C	10 min. 20 min. 45 min.	10–12%	Butane torch/programmable electric kiln. For PMC3 with glass, fire from cold kiln.
PMC Sheet (also known as PMC Paper)	Fire from cold kiln 1650°F/900°C 1560°F/850°C 1472°F/800°C	10 min. 20 min. 30 min.	10–15%	Programmable electric kiln
PMC+ Sheet	1650°F/900°C 1560°F/850°C 1472°F/800°C	10 min. 20 min. 30 min.	10–15%	Programmable electric kiln
PMC also known as PMC Standard	1650°F/900°C	2 hours	25–30%	Programmable electric kiln

Equipment

Drying equipment

Metal clay needs to be completely dry before it can be fired, otherwise moisture in the clay will cause cracks or even breaks. The simplest way to dry pieces is to let them set overnight, but you can hasten the drying time by using the following items.

A **griddle** set to the lowest possible temperature (about 150°F/66°C) helps ensure even drying of flat pieces. Place pieces on the surface and turn them over occasionally. Most pieces will dry within 20–25 minutes. Look for a uniform light coloration – dark areas indicate moisture is still present, which could crack the piece if fired prematurely. (A cup warmer makes an inexpensive drying device for one or two pieces.) For three-dimensional pieces, use a **food dehydrator**. Thorough drying may take 30 minutes or more, depending on the thickness of the clay and the complexity of the piece. A food dehydrator also is good for drying leaves and seed pods before covering them with slip.

Firing equipment

A small, programmable **electric kiln** fires pieces, burning away the organic binder to transform metal clay into fine silver or gold. Items in the kiln rest on a shelf.

Always use **tongs** to place items in a preheated kiln and to remove items from a hot kiln.

A **butane torch**, the same kind used in making crème brûlée, can be used to fire small pieces (no larger than a dime) made from PMC3.

Vermiculite supports dimensional pieces, allowing them to retain their shape during firing. To hold the vermiculite, use small, inexpensive ceramic dishes because they will crack after one or two firings.

Finishing equipment

When metal clay is fired, it turns white. Polishing removes the white layer, leaving the shiny silver surface. Brushing the fired piece with a steel brush and soapy water works, but if you want faster results, use one of the following devices.

A **rotary tumbler-polisher** polishes pieces with stainless-steel shot and polishing solution. Most pieces require no more than 30 minutes to achieve a high level of shine.

A **magnetic polisher** gives a superior polish in less time than a rotary tumbler because it uses polishing media, which are smaller than shot and able to get into tiny spaces for a more even polish.

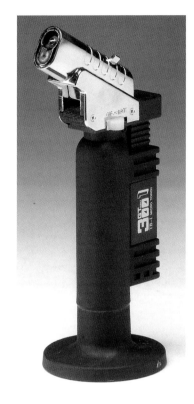

Butane torch

Vermiculite in ceramic saucer; programmable electric kiln

Tips and techniques

Keeping the clay moist

The lump form of metal clay dries out quickly, so make every effort to keep it moist and malleable. Remove only what you need from the package, and immediately wrap the remaining portion in plastic wrap. Keep a mister handy while you're working with it and spritz the clay from time to time to keep it fresh.

To keep syringe clay fresh, always store an opened syringe tip-down in a cup of water.

It's always a good idea to keep a cup of water, a brush, and a paper towel at your side while working with metal clay.

Rolling out the clay

To roll out metal clay, lightly grease a plastic mat and roller. Place the clay on the mat between two equal stacks of cards. If you wish, you may place an extra plastic mat over the clay to help it retain moisture. Be sure the ends of the roller always rest on the cards to ensure the clay will be rolled evenly.

Working with casting grain

Many metal clay pieces are embellished with casting grain. Attach these little balls of precious metal with syringe clay. I generally use silver casting grain, but it also is available in other metals, including 24k gold, rose gold, and copper.

Handling with care

Once the clay has dried, it can be fragile. Work gently and carefully when filing, adding holes, and sanding. Do the majority of your sanding before firing the piece; dry, unfired clay is much easier to sand than fired clay. Pay special attention to sanding the insides of rings to make them smooth.

To avoid wasting clay, hold pieces that you are sanding over slip of the same type of clay. The clay dust will settle into the slip.

Signing your piece

If you wish to sign your piece or add your initials, use a needle stylus to sign it before firing. Lightly scratch the surface and then go over it again once or twice, removing a small amount of clay.

What can be fired in a kiln

Cubic zirconias (CZs) and synthetic corundums can be fired in the kiln at any of the recommended temperatures for any PMC product.

Glass cabochons, including dichroic glass, can be fired in the kiln with PMC3 products only at the recommended temperatures for PMC3. Most glass begins to flow at around 1400°F (760°C), and therefore it is not recommended that you use PMC+ products with glass. However, if the glass flowing is part of the design, then you might want to experiment.

Porcelain can be fired in the kiln at any of the temperatures recommended for PMC products. Because the glazes used on porcelain may have different reactions at higher temperatures, it's safer to fire at lower temperatures or test-fire an extra glazed piece like the one you're planning to use.

Adding a patina

Liver of sulfur can add a lovely antique finish or colorful shine to your metal clay pieces. It comes in two forms: dry chunks in a can or ready-to-use liquid. A little goes a long way, so buy a minimal quantity and use it sparingly. I like to use the dry form, as it stays fresher for a longer period of time.

Though liver of sulfur is nontoxic, its powerful odor of rotten eggs can be unpleasant. Use it in a well-ventilated room and avoid inhaling the fumes.

To add a patina, take a small chunk of liver of sulfur and place it in just enough hot water to cover your metal clay piece. When the liver of sulfur has melted, use tweezers to dip your piece in the solution. You'll see colors begin to appear, and when the piece is a color that you like, remove it and rinse with cold running water. You can use a polishing cloth or pad to remove some of the patina.

Each batch of liver of sulfur produces different results. I generally patina a piece, see what colors result, and then choose beads to complement the patina. If you aren't happy with the results, you can re-fire the piece or use a tarnish remover to take off the patina and try again.

Working with syringe clay

When using syringe, controlling it can be a challenge. I've found the best way is to let ¼ to ½ in. of syringe dangle from the end of the tip [a] and simply let it drop in place onto your piece [b]. You always can nudge it slightly with a wet brush [c]. To make a dot or blob, touch the syringe to the piece and squeeze out clay to the size you want [d]. If you're having difficulty stopping the syringe flow, you can use a needle stylus to break it.

Syringes come filled and ready to use. Keep your syringes tip-down in water whenever they are not in use.

a

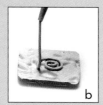
b

c

d

Resources

Eclectica, Inc.
Galleria West Shopping Center
18900 W. Bluemound Rd., #142-148
Brookfield, WI 53045
262-641-0910
eclecticabeads.com

My store, Eclectica, carries beads from around the world as well as all of the PMC products, tools, and accessories you will need to make the projects in this book. We provide a wide variety of beading and metal clay classes.

The Bead Studio
Galleria West Shopping Center
18900 W. Bluemound Rd., #139
Brookfield, WI 53045
262-641-0961

The Bead Studio offers beading kits, studio time and tool rental, kiln-firing services, and space for private parties.

PMC Connection
3718 Cavalier Dr.
Garland, TX 75042
866-762-2529
pmcconnection.com

PMC Connection sells a full range of PMC products, tools, and accessories. The Web site also provides a listing of certified instructors nationwide. If you are interested in certification, use the site to look for certification workshops in your area.

Beadissimo
1051 Valencia St.
San Francisco, CA 94110
415-282-2323
beadissimo.com

This store sells PMC products, tools, and accessories. A comprehensive class schedule includes beading, wirework, PMC, metalworking, and glass beadmaking instruction.

The Bead Factory
3019 6th Ave.
Tacoma, WA 98406
888-500-BEAD
thebeadfactory.com

This 5,000-square-foot store carries thousands of beads, PMC products and tools, and other jewelry-making items. Classes cover everything from basic beading and wirework to PMC and glass beadmaking.

Brighton Beads & More
9850 E. Grand River Ave.
Brighton, MI 48116
810-844-0066
brightonbeadsandmore.com

This family-run store offers a great selection of classes on PMC and glass fusing.

About the author
Irina Miech was born in Kiev, Ukraine. She pursued degrees in international relations and Russian but became interested in beading while running an import business that dealt in Moroccan jewelry and handicrafts. She began designing her own jewelry and selling it through galleries and museum shops. She opened her bead store, Eclectica (eclecticabeads.com), in 1993 and has been teaching beading and jewelry-making classes there since then. She began teaching Precious Metal Clay classes as a Certified Instructor in 2002, and became a PMC Senior Instructor in 2005. Her beading, jewelry, and metal clay designs have been featured in *Bead&Button*, *BeadStyle*, and *Art Jewelry* magazines.
    Irina lives in Brookfield, Wis., with her husband and two sons.

Acknowledgments
I would like to thank Tony Miech for his constant support of my work, Lauren Matusko for her writing advice, and my sons, Zachary and David, for all the pods, leaves, shells, and their unconditional love and encouragement. I would also like to thank my wonderful store staff for their support, enthusiasm, and willingness to help in all my undertakings.